My Father and Me

KATIA FLORENCIO PARKER

Copyright © 2023 by Katia Florencio Parker.

All rights reserved. No part of this book may be reproduced, stored, or transmitted by any means—whether auditory, graphic, mechanical, or electronic—without written permission of both publisher and author, except in the case of brief excerpts used in critical articles and reviews. Unauthorized reproduction of any part of this work is illegal and is punishable by law.

All the characters' names are fictitious. The names of places such as Rancho Aurora and Farmácia Brilho do Sol are fictitious as well. The names of some cities, such as Monte Feliz and Santana, are also fictitious. Some other city names are real, such as Salvador, Petrolina, and Juazeiro. The author reserves the rights of her own narrative of this book.

Library of Congress Control Number: 2016902020

ISBN: 979-8-89031-453-6 (sc)
ISBN: 979-8-89031-454-3 (hc)
ISBN: 979-8-89031-455-0 (e)

Because of the dynamic nature of the Internet, any web addresses or links contained in this book may have changed since publication and may no longer be valid. The views expressed in this work are solely those of the author and do not necessarily reflect the views of the publisher, and the publisher hereby disclaims any responsibility for them.

One Galleria Blvd., Suite 1900, Metairie, LA 70001
(504) 702-6708
1-888-421-2397

To my father (in memoriam),
for the inspiration to pursue my dreams.

To my mother, for her faith in God and the angels.
Her memories of the past are gone. I'm glad she told me her story.

To my sons, for giving me hope to continue the journey of my life.

And in his last days he said:
"The day that you die, you won't feel anything." And he died the next day.

CONTENTS

Chapter 1   The Cry of the Heart 1

Chapter 2   The Passing 7

Chapter 3   The Secret 14

Chapter 4   Rancho Aurora 20

Chapter 5   The Flight of the Eagles 28

Chapter 6   The Good Samaritan 40

Chapter 7   The Fall of the Bedroom Wall... 46

Chapter 8   The Roller Coaster of the Mind 51

Chapter 9   The Survival...56

Chapter 10 The Will 64

Chapter 11 The Road to Heaven 72

Chapter 12 The Inheritance..79

CHAPTER 1

The Cry of the Heart

The year was 1970. The last day of the year, the *Reveillon*, was just days ahead, and my future sister-in-law, Amanda (my oldest brother's fiancée), had come from her hometown to spend Christmas and the last days of the year with us. I felt so excited to go to the club with my oldest brother and future sister-in-law and spend the Reveillon having a good time, as we usually had in the past. We usually had New Year's Eve dinner with our family, and then we would go to the club. Actually, this would be just my second time going to Feira Tennis Clube at midnight for the *Reveillon*, which is a word borrowed from the French language and incorporated into the Portuguese language that we understand as meaning "waking up." As a tradition, people gather in the club much before midnight, and then they dance and have fun as they celebrate the passing of the old year and the beginning of the New Year.

It was glamorous. After midnight, the music the band played changed from romantic and slow to the more exciting rhythms of Mardi Gras music or, as we called it, Carnival rhythms. Confetti and streamers were all over the club, and always everyone got a glass of champagne at exactly midnight. This was perhaps the best day of the year for the young people and for the old ones as well. On this day, everybody enjoyed the party, as it marked the arrival of the New Year, and the celebration continued until the band stopped at the first light of the sun.

* * *

Let me introduce myself. My name is Katia Florencio. My married name is Katia Florencio Parker. I have a story to tell. Sit down; just read and relax. Imagine that you are watching a movie—a very exciting movie with an intriguing, very real betrayal covered in pretension, authority, fear, money, bitterness, and compassion. However, in the end, there will be forgiveness—forgiveness because destiny twists everything and everybody learns from each other and also from the consequences of the betrayal.

This story is a recollection of a father's life, his daughter's sorrows, all his children's lives, his wife's life, and the life of his ambitious lover Daniela and briefly a series of short stories about his last lover, Iracema, and her child. It portrays flashbacks into the lives of three families and the patriarch, André Florencio, my father. In writing this story, I recall the writings and romantic poems of Shakespeare, which are spiced with love, romance, and betrayal.

I come from a family of six, but I should say that at home, there were five of us: my mother, Diana; my brothers, Ernesto, Eric, and André; and me, the youngest in the family. My father did not live with us. That's the reason for my story: a sad child missed her father. She respected his authority; sometimes she feared him, or we all did—my brothers and I. There is so much to say about our lives. I am the one who decided to write about our lives because I suppose my brothers decided to forget. I feel that I pretended for too long, all my childhood and teenage years.

As a child, a teenager, and a young woman, I enjoyed life. I graduated from high school and a state college, and I am grateful to my father for my education. When he passed away unexpectedly, I had just completed my first year of high school.

In this book, I might be controversial as I express myself with regard to my father. I really loved and respected him; however, many times as a child and a teenager, I felt that I had to pretend that I was happy and that everything was fine when it wasn't. For example, I had to accept his absence in our house. The reality was that he lived in a different house with his other family. On holidays, sometimes he would stay at his ranch and we wouldn't see him.

I used to wonder, *What is my father doing at night on his ranch with his other family?* and I answered myself, *He is probably having dinner or watching TV with his other children, sharing stories, talking and laughing, simply being there with them.* During these moments, my mother, my brothers, and I would miss him. At our home, we learned how to live without him.

My father was not a rude man—actually, he was very nice to people. I know that he was a charismatic person, as I used to watch him talk to customers in his pharmacy. He was very polite, and he always offered to help someone in need. However, my father, by personality, was always too busy doing one thing or the other. From a very young age, I would hear him say to his employees at the pharmacy, "I have to go back to the ranch; I might not come back today because I left some people repairing the barn and I have to talk to the workers." Then I knew he would be with his other family for the rest of the day. Then he would take me home and drive to his ranch, and the day was over.

My father was always busy with life inside and outside of his pharmacy. He used to divide his time between his ranch and his pharmacy. At his ranch, he always had something to do. I think my father never noticed that this kind of situation was frustrating for me and my brothers deep inside. I felt I needed courage to tell him that everything was unfair. I would smile, pretending that everything was okay. The truth is at home we felt betrayed. We never said the word *betrayal* to my father because we did not want to hurt his feelings. Although my brothers and I were his first family, life did not prove to be that way. From a very young age, my mother, my brothers, and I lived in three rental houses before my father finally bought a house for us. There is a story about that in a later chapter.

My family is from the state of Bahia, the most beautiful state in Brazil, where birds fly free over large areas of green forests, along running rivers and peaceful lakes. Many rivers meet the blue seawater, and together, the sweet and salty waters mix to form the vast ocean, and then the ocean expands and life goes on.

In my childhood, I was told that God brought us into this world and we are intelligent beings able to learn how to balance and synchronize our lives and our surroundings. I was taught to treat people well and I would be treated well for my good deeds. As a child and a teenager, I learned that we have to make our own happiness. I learned at home that we have to cope with unpredictable times. I recall that some days I really wanted to be a child forever because I knew that grown-ups have serious responsibilities; they have to grow up, work, and have families, and grown-ups have to survive despite difficult circumstances, and this was a child's fear. Psychologically, kids naturally go through this stage of their lives.

My mother, my brothers, and I lived knowing that something was missing in our house, and it was my father. Growing up, the five of us at home realized that we had to swim according to the sea. The waters were unpredictable, but we were in the boat and we needed our father to live. Growing up without a father in the house every day and every night and having to walk to his pharmacy every morning to ask for his blessing were unfair for me.

I was perhaps thirteen years old when one day in his pharmacy, we started a conversation about the past. I asked him why he left us. He answered that at the time, he was not happy. Deep inside, as a teenager, I understood his words, but I really did not accept them. He was trying to tell me that he was not complete. Yet, in my understanding, his first children at home had to suffer because in life, sometimes things don't turn the way we plan in the beginning, and life goes on. Also, I recall the day I did not have the courage to tell him, "You and my mother really did not know each other." Then again I thought, *When you met your employee Daniela, did you think that you finally had found what you were looking for?* All these things crossed my mind; however, again, I did not have the courage to say to him what I was really thinking and feeling.

My father's pharmacy was where he felt he could have all his children together, as that place was like his house—his own home. It did not belong to Diana, our mother, or Daniela, his companion, the mother of his other children. It was just his, and having this place, his children would not feel jealous of each other. He wouldn't be in his other house, which was actually Daniela's house, the one he worked hard to build.

The first time my father took me to his ranch, which he named Rancho Aurora, I was about five years old. I looked down at the driveway, and I read the words "Daniela e filhos," which in English translate to "Daniela and children." As a child, immediately I sensed Daniela's intentions. A very young child has intuition. Although I was very young, at five years old, I was a good reader. Then, after that, every time he took me to the ranch, I would look at those words carved into the cement: "Daniela e filhos."

When I was fourteen years old, I had more intuition, and I would tell myself, *Daniela intentionally engraved those words as a message for the Oliveira Florencios, my brothers and me, to make sure we understood that the house belonged just to her and her children.* The message Daniela tried to convey was ironic, selfish, and ambitious. Those words were there to compensate for an empty space in Daniela's life: the lack of her own father. I used to think, *Why did my father permit this? If it is their house, why are those words engraved in the cement?* Those words remained in the driveway for many, many years.

Reflections are flashbacks, and I want to tell my father's story and give my recollections of a very interesting, enigmatic, and charismatic man who lived his life always looking for self-fulfillment and his own happiness. Also, I want to record recollections of those who were touched by his life: his wife, his children, his companion, and his last lover.

Not so long ago, I had a dream that I had written a book, and the book was exactly like this one. Did I have a premonition? Perhaps. When I woke up, I told myself, *I want to write a book. That's what I will do. I will let my imagination soar. I will let the child, the teenager, and the young woman come back and tell their stories.* Those versions of myself are here as kinetic energy. A past that nobody can see anymore still exists; therefore, I will tell my story in flashbacks as recollections of the past.

Perhaps someone has lived a similar life and we share emotions. Here are my childhood memories—memories with happiness, sorrow, betrayal, reconciliation, and forgiveness. Perhaps I should say everything that happened was for a reason, and the reason was to learn—to learn how to survive.

CHAPTER 2

The Passing

On Thursday, December 24, 1970, my father decided to celebrate his mother's eightieth birthday with a lunch on the small farm where she lived with my aunt Janete. My aunt Janete was not my grandmother's daughter. She actually was my mother's sister, and she had three children. Her two youngest children, Aline and Lucas, lived with her. The reality is that my aunt Janete really needed to move from the city in which she had lived since she got married, as now she was separated and things were not going well with her husband. Despite all the problems he had with my mother—and despite their separation causing us so much sorrow—my father somehow was a compassionate man. So he dealt with my aunt Janete, asking her to come to Santana and take care of his mother in exchange for him providing her with a small ranch house, all expenses paid; this meant my aunt Janete would take care of my grandmother perhaps for the last days of her life.

My grandmother suffered from arteriosclerosis, and it seemed that my father, André Florencio, an experienced pharmacist, knew his mother's medical condition meant she would not live too long. Destiny twisted the good days we planned to have. The day after my grandmother's birthday, which had been a happy celebration, my father fell ill. My father always came downtown to open the pharmacy. My brothers would come help him if he really needed help. He used to open the pharmacy on Sundays just for a few hours while we were at church so he could somehow make some money, and then after church services, he would take us back to his pharmacy. Sometimes, Ernesto and Eric, being the older brothers, would drive us to the church, and then after the services, they would drive us back to the pharmacy.

When we carried out this plan on Sundays, by noon, my father would close the pharmacy, and he would drive my brothers and I home. We lived in downtown Santana until I was about eleven. Then he would drive back to the ranch, taking his other children with him. My father and Daniela had lived in this ranch for the past fifteen years. There, they raised their children: David, Fernando, Samantha, Lívia, and Eliana. All my half-brothers and half-sisters had the surname Florencio, as my brothers and I, his first children with my mother, Diana, did. He bought this huge ranch not so far from the ranch my grandmother lived between 1954 and 1955.

* * *

The morning my father fell ill was quite unreal. He had never complained about chest pain or any other serious physical condition before. When I was at the pharmacy, I can remember him telling my siblings and I and his employees that his liver sometimes acted up. He had, according to his own diagnosis, light liver pain, so he would just take Litrison, pink capsules that he believed would make the discomfort go away.

That Sunday morning, my oldest brother, Ernesto, had told my father that he would come to the pharmacy to help him because Ernesto had been away at the agricultural college. Actually, on Sundays, my father was not really busy. Sundays were quiet, so Ernesto and my father had time to talk. For some reason, that day, we did not go to church. Perhaps my father had told Ernesto that he wanted to rest longer before staying at the pharmacy until noon.

Because Ernesto was not living in town at this time, we hadn't been going to church as before. Ernesto had just graduated from college, and he was planning to get a job as an agricultural engineer and eventually marry Amanda. During his four years of college, he had lived in the city of Juazeiro da Bahia across from Petrolina, which was in the state of Pernambuco. The San Francisco River separates these two states, so the college is called Faculdade de Agricultura do Médio São Francisco, which in English means "the College of Agriculture of the Middle San Francisco River."

When Ernesto approached the pharmacy, he saw that it was closed. He immediately walked to Senhor Francisco, the shoe man who had a shoe-shine business, which was on the corner by my father's pharmacy. Ernesto asked him where my father was. Ernesto sensed that something was not right. Senhor Francisco told Ernesto that my father had told him he was not feeling well and he had to close the pharmacy so he could drive himself to a local hospital, as he could not breathe well. Ernesto took a taxi, briefly explaining the situation to the taxi driver, telling him that he wanted to check the two hospitals in town, as my father would be in one of the two, probably the one not so far from the pharmacy.

When the taxi reached the first hospital, Ernesto ran to the front entrance and explained the situation to a nurse he saw. She told him to ask the receptionist in the front lobby. When he asked for André Florencio, the young lady told him that less than an hour before, a man named André Florencio had come in complaining of chest pain. She told Ernesto, "Please go to room 72."

Ernesto walked down the hallway. Then he stopped and saw room 72. When he opened the door, he found my father lying down. He asked my dad, "Pai, que aconteceu?" which in English means, "Dad, what happened?" Then he added, "Ontem o senhor estava tão feliz e se sentindo bem, quando todos nós estávamos celebrando o aniversário de Vovó, e hoje eu encontro o senhor aqui ..." In English, that translates to "Yesterday, you were so happy, and well, when we all were celebrating Grandmom's birthday, and today I find you here ..." Ernesto was shaking; he feared something really serious was happening to him.

My father responded, "I think that my liver wants to scare me." Then a doctor came in and told Ernesto that he was not sure what had happened. Yet another doctor prescribed him a strong pain reliever. The hospital did not have the technology of today's hospitals even in that town of one hundred thousand people at the time.

Ernesto drove my father to his ranch and kept his car. The next morning, he drove back to the ranch. My father was still complaining about his mysterious pain. He kept saying to Ernesto that he would be okay—that the problem was just his liver. He told Ernesto that he probably had just eaten something bad during his mom's birthday dinner, perhaps too much *pimenta malagueta* (jalapeno pepper) and that was the cause of his liver pain.

All day, Ernesto stayed at the ranch, preoccupied. Our half-brothers were much younger than Ernesto. Eliana, Daniela's youngest child, was just five years old. Daniela was in shock. So many things crossed her mind. What if my father was having heart problems, as he had never felt this way before? Ernesto then came back to our house and told my mother, Eric, André, and I what was happening at the ranch. Deep inside, Ernesto feared for my father's condition.

The next morning, on Tuesday, my father's chest pain continued. My father kept telling Daniela and Ernesto that he would be okay. He just needed to rest and to sleep. Ernesto said that, instead, he needed to take him to the hospital. My father rejected that idea. He told Ernesto to wait one more day.

Ernesto brought Sabrina to the pharmacy. Sabrina was an Afro-Brazilian young woman; somehow, she was my father's protégé. My father had met Sabrina in a tiny city where, at the time, he had opened a small pharmacy, and Sabrina was looking for a job. She barely had an education—just elementary school. However, she was a smart young woman. My father had told Daniela a few years before that he was planning to bring a young lady he met to live with them. Sabrina's mother had died, and her father had begged my father to have compassion for her. When my father brought Sabrina to the ranch to live with his second family, I never could be sure that Daniela agreed to it or not. My father always had the last word. I believe he decided to bring her and that Daniela just had to accept it. I guess Daniela did not like too many of his ideas, yet Sabrina lived in the ranch house with them for many years—actually, until he died.

So my father brought the young Sabrina to work in his pharmacy and taught her how to manage the pharmacy. The pharmacy was my father's business. That was where he made the money to provide all of us, his two families, with our living. If he had to travel for a few days, Sabrina managed the pharmacy, as he trusted her, and in his absence, everything ran smoothly. Perhaps it was a way to control expenses, rather than hiring another person, since she lived with them, and I believe he thought that Sabrina would never betray him for any reason if he had to be away from the pharmacy. Sabrina was the perfect person to manage his business.

The next morning, Ernesto drove to the farm and found out that my father had been in great pain all night long. After managing to get my father into the car, Daniela, Sabrina, and Ernesto took him to the hospital. Ernesto stopped briefly at the pharmacy, where he dropped off Sabrina so she could open the pharmacy. Then he rushed Daniela and our father to the hospital, the one my father had checked himself into.

At the hospital, Ernesto talked to the physician who had attended to him on Sunday, and the physician decided to run some X-rays. They did not have the ultrasound or meticulous scan technology that exists nowadays. After some X-rays, the physician told Ernesto, "Your father is having chest pains. You must take him immediately to a better hospital in Salvador for a better checkup and treatment." I recall at that time, people in that city did not have medical insurance. If needed, people would just pay cash for any medical expenses. The poor would just go to a public hospital, while middle-class people always had a general-practice doctor who somehow was a friend. If a member of someone's family got sick, the family's doctor would take care of him or her, and the doctor would get paid for those services, and that was it.

After my father got X-rayed, the physician again explained to Ernesto that my father needed to be taken to Salvador, as his pain was increasing. He repeated that his condition was serious. The two hospitals in Santana did not have the advanced technology to really pinpoint the serious state of my father's condition, and his condition was not getting any better. Ernesto started to make plans to drive my father to the capital. However, my father refused to leave the city. Ernesto insisted on telling him that in Santana, the hospitals did not have the technology to treat him. The doctors could not treat him or operate on him. In town, there were no heart specialists to really diagnose his serious condition. I can't say for sure what crossed his mind when he heard this.

The clock was ticking. At the time, I was sixteen years old. I was somehow naïve of life's ups and downs. I had a boyfriend, and at the time, I felt happy, as my nineteen-year-old boyfriend was very much a friend. As far as I can recollect, I was not aware of how serious his condition was. Everything happened so fast. He had not had heart problems before, or if he did, he had experienced them in secret.

And even Daniela did not imagine how serious the situation was. My father stayed in the hospital. I remember that he slept for two days straight. The doctors kept him on medication that made him sleep all day and all night on Wednesday and Thursday. On the morning of Friday, January 1, 1971, I went to the hospital with my sister-in-law Amanda. My father woke up and asked us, "What day is today?"

Amanda responded, "Senhor André, today is Friday."

Then he said, "The day you die, you won't feel anything. I feel like I died and I came back to life. I don't remember anything that happened these last two days." This was like a premonition for his passing the next day.

On Saturday morning, Daniela was by his side. She had been in the hospital with him all night long. She was exhausted, yet she had not left him alone. She had not slept, since he hadn't either. I believe that Daniela wanted to believe everything would be fine and that this situation was just a bad, bad dream. I know she was afraid—very afraid—something worse was coming. If she could do anything to relieve him of this pain, she would. She sensed the pain he was feeling. Then, as Ernesto told me later, our father began feeling short of breath. Daniela screamed, and the physician and a nurse in charge of him came in to assess the situation. They tried to help him to breathe. Another doctor as well as another nurse came in. They tried to control the situation, yet he was gone.

We came to know that he had a myocardial infarction, a massive heart attack. His heart stopped. They tried to resuscitate him, yet it was not possible. His heart had been slowly swelling for days. Daniela screamed knowing that he was leaving her forever. One of the nurses called Ernesto and told him to come to the hospital immediately, as our father had just passed away. The difficult part for Ernesto was informing Eric and André, who were not in town and who did not know about our father's condition, as he had asked Ernesto not to call them because they were a few days away from taking a college entrance test in Salvador. My father thought that not telling Eric and André about his situation would save them from tension and preoccupation while the boys were doing so much preparation for the difficult college entrance test.

Finally, Ernesto called Eric and André, asking them to come back to town immediately, and told them what happened: our father had passed away. He quickly explained that it was our father's decision not to make them aware of his condition. Eric and André quickly got on a bus from Salvador to Santana, which was just two hours away by bus. When they arrived in Santana, Ernesto went to the bus station to bring them home.

My father's body was taken to Rancho Aurora, as he loved that place where he lived for so long. It was his home, it was his ranch, and I recall many times when he told me that Rancho Aurora was like a paradise. And I could understand him. He had planted so many fruit trees; he had put so much money into that place. For him, it was like heaven. That was the way I felt and I still feel; during his lifetime, that place really filled his soul and spirit. In South America even today, as far as I know, hospitals do not embalm corpses. Families must arrange funeral services for the day after a loved one passes away.

My father's passing was unbelievable. Everything happened so fast. Even today, I feel his presence, as when he was alive. As days passed after his death, my mother would tell us that he was with God and that he was in peace. We all prayed for him at home every day, and we all felt his presence in his last pharmacy, Farmácia Brilho do Sol, which in English translates to "Sunshine Pharmacy." I guess Daniela must have felt his presence in Rancho Aurora as well. Sometimes, I think that he is there, walking invisibly and taking care of what he loved so much. Many times, he told me, "Rancho Aurora is my paradise," and I always knew that it was and maybe still is his paradise, even in heaven.

CHAPTER 3

The reality is that André Florencio, my father, never had enemies. Ironically, after he died, my mother, Diana, and his lover, Daniela, both were left with feelings of love and betrayal.

My mother, a woman without a formal education, almost lost her mind when he left her in November 1953 while she was pregnant with me. He left us to open his new pharmacy in Santana and start his new life with Daniela, his new lover and companion. My father promised my mother that he would come back in a few months to take us to Santana. He would rent a house for her and the children. He explained to her that he had to set up things; he had to open a pharmacy, make money, and, first of all, rent a place to live for him and Daniela. My mother found it hard to swallow his words, as it was a surprise. What a surprise.

My mother told me that he mentioned she could talk to her brother about this, as he couldn't talk to him about his unexpected decision to leave her. However, it seemed that he had been planning this move for at least a year. No doubt about that. My uncle, my mother's brother, waited a long time for my father's decision to bring us to Santana. At the time, my uncle became an angel for my mother and us, and finally, eighteen long months after my father left, he dealt with my father, telling him he had to bring us to Santana because it was becoming very difficult for my mother to be alone with us kids without resources. And mostly, he told my father it was difficult for us to not have our father and husband's emotional support.

It's hard to believe that my mother waited alone with her children, without him by her side, for so long. In Portuguese, there is an expression that describes situations like this. We say, "We have to eat the bread that the devil prepared." And that is exactly what happened. I believe that my mother's sister Janete and my grandfather Leonardo held my mother's soul so she wouldn't fall. The wait was long. For all of us, it became a long, long journey. Just God knows how she managed to stay sane. While I was growing up, she would tell me that as a Catholic woman, she really believed that God would not leave her alone—that he would take care of all of us: her and her children.

More than one and a half years after my father left his wife and children—my brothers and I—we finally moved. Eleven months had passed since I was born. Then finally we went to Santana, the city where my father had been living with Daniela. My uncle Joel had been living in this city as well. My uncle had dealt with my father and determined that he would drive us from Monte Feliz, as he could not wait for my father's decision on when we would move. Daniela was pregnant with David, her first child. My uncle knew that my father would be busy, with another baby on the way. My mother would set up her life with my brothers and me in a rental house in a new city. Being in the city where my father was living, she would finally have some support financially and emotionally.

When we arrived in Santana, according to my mother's recollections, my father had the pharmacy open and he had already bought a huge ranch named Rancho Aurora. I guess he was doing well. He had bought this ranch while we were alone in Monte Feliz. As soon as we arrived from Monte Feliz, my father told Ernesto, who was nine years old at the time, that he had plans to build a ranch house. He knew that he and Daniela would eventually have more children. He told Ernesto that he would plant lots of fruit trees and, in a few more years, Ernesto, Eric, André, and I, Katia, could come to the ranch on some Sundays; enjoy time under the mango, orange, and guava trees; and see the animals he would have on the ranch.

Today, as I write this memoir, I wonder if my father asked Ernesto about how he, Eric, André, and my mother had lived and also, after my birth, how we had survived without him for eighteen months. Perhaps he did not say anything; maybe he thought that he could compensate from that moment on. Even though we knew that life has its ups and downs, we never thought that my father would die so young, at just forty-six years old.

* * *

Later, recollecting the day of his funeral, my sister-in-law Amanda told me that among the attending people, a young countrywoman dressed in black came to see him for the last time. Amanda asked me if I had noticed. I answered, "No, I didn't."

Amanda said that the woman had cried as if she was a member of the family. Then I asked Amanda, "Was she the farm lover?" The previous year, one day while at home, I overheard something Ernesto said to my mother. At the time, I guess I did not ask questions.

Amanda knew that I was confused. Then she confirmed my suspicion: "Yes, Katia, she is, or perhaps I can say that she was your father's lover." It was a surprise, at least for me. At the time, I felt very confused about my father's newest romance, and moreover, I found out that when he died, he and the supposed new lover had a very young son. Amanda knew that the little boy had just had his first birthday.

It was so sad that my father never told us about his little boy. My father died on January 2, and his youngest son had his first birthday on New Year's Day of 1971. It was life's irony, like destiny's irony. How would Shakespeare write about this love triangle? "And he had a wife, a lover—companion and, at the end, another lover"?

I thought about the little boy. When Amanda told me about my father's secret, I really felt compassion for the little child and somehow for his mother as well. I had not been aware of this third family. He never told me about this countrywoman. As I said, I overheard things, yet before he died, he never told me about this third family he had. It was his secret.

I recalled that sometimes he used to tell me there were certain things in life that he, as a man, could do. If I am not wrong, he said that a woman could not do these things. He did not explain it to me clearly; it sounded like an enigma. I really believe he tried to say that he, as a man, had some kind of freedom to do things that his daughters did not have. Thinking about this, I questioned myself. I silently asked myself, *Well, my father is trying to say that he has the freedom to do certain things, but freedom to do what?* His words were, as I said, enigmatic.

After the funeral, when I found out about his third family, for me, the entire story was still a real enigma. Even today, I am confused when I think about that conversation with my father. I could not understand what he tried to tell me. Well, he betrayed my mother, and then he betrayed Daniela. I think perhaps he had implied that he, as a man, could date or live with another woman but that it had to be behind his companion Daniela's back. What other explanation could he have?

At the time, there was no other explanation. Always, I believed that my father was a good man, and I know he was; however, he accepted certain things just for himself. Sometimes it seemed that he lived according to his own laws. That was not fair. I think that after living with Daniela for sixteen years and having five children with her, something ignited inside him and he started to feel lonely, so he looked for a new companion. Perhaps he felt Daniela was not fulfilling his soul and spirit anymore. I remember my father telling me more than once that Daniela was a very smart woman, then after knowing about the countrywoman story, this contradicted the idea he left my mother because she was too naïve. But then, years later, life proved that Daniela's smart traits weren't enough. This confession, according to my mother, triggered his heart condition.

It seemed that my father had flaws and he tended to go for women much younger than he was. He was too old involving himself with a much younger woman. He was about forty-three years old when he met this nineteen-year-old country girl. She was the daughter of a farmer—actually, the daughter of one of his farm employees. Anyway, this young woman eventually became his third lover. He did not live with her. This was his last secret.

Three years before my father passed away, he bought a new farm, and he began this new romance. I recall my mother and I spending some time on the farm. We spent a week there on summer vacations. Summer in Brazil is during the months of December, January, and February. I recall that he would leave the pharmacy on Wednesday and he used to say, "I am raising cattle on the new farm," I suppose as an additional business and a hobby. Then he would come back on Thursday afternoon. So a romance did go on, perhaps since buying the farm.

Why did he decide to buy this farm far away from where we all lived? It took him at least three hours to reach the new place. Perhaps he did it to get away from Daniela and because my mother had not been part of his life anymore for so long. When he bought the farm, did he premeditate that he would meet someone? I don't know. It seems that he felt the need to get away from his two families and his business for one or two days per week to live a new kind of "adventure."

Long after his passing, I came to know certain facts that helped me make sense of his secret existence; I don't know exactly when and how the romance started, but it seems that he started this romance when I was just thirteen years old—actually, when he bought the big farm away from Santana. This place was about one hundred miles from Santana. The farm neighbored a small farm owned by one of his employees, who was the grandfather of his new son. So this was where his third family lived. I believe that Ernesto, my oldest brother, knew about our father's secret rendezvous.

All along, the pharmacy was like his home. It was more than his business place. It was not Daniela's house, nor my mother Diana's house; it was just for him and his children. He loved his pharmacy. He loved the ranch where he lived with Daniela and their children. He acquired his first paradise in 1954 or 1955. A few years later, he built Daniela's dream house.

By the time he died, he had ten children with three women, yet he was still officially married to my mother. My mother did not believe in divorce nor accept it. A separation was already a great sin and humiliation. Imagine giving your husband a divorce so the other woman could become the wife and you, the ex-wife, would be a single woman. For the Catholic Italians in Brazil, a separation was already a recipe for a big disaster that eventually would come. So a Catholic Italian wife held her marriage like a gold cross as a symbol of pride, honor, and hope—a hope that perhaps one day her husband would come back and the past would be forgotten like a bad dream. However, the wife would really see reality after waking from her dream. Her revenge was that she would hold her ring, hold her marriage certificate, and the lover would *never* become a legal wife. The other one could live with the husband forever yet be the illegal mistress. This was the revenge of the Catholic Italian woman in this country.

In old times, the Italians as well as the Portuguese descendants were Catholic, so they followed the same religion, the same way of thinking. For them, the mistress would perhaps be just a forever lover called the "other one," never a legal wife. What could the abandoned woman do to the husband after the humiliation she had gone through? This was the only revenge.

My mother had a story like this one. She never signed any papers that were brought to her when I was nine or ten years old. Perhaps my father had tried when I was much younger. I don't have recollections, or she never told me. But I recall my father asked Ernesto to talk to my mother about the advantages of a separation, and I recall that Ernesto brought her the separation papers that my father had probably arranged for a lawyer to prepare. I recall hearing Ernesto telling my mother that my father would give her a certain amount of money. I believe that Ernesto was innocently talking to my mother without knowing the implications of a separation.

These papers were crafted like in the preparation of a literary essay, which must be drafted, edited, and then carefully prepared as a final copy to deliver to the teacher. In this particular situation, the lawyer prepared the final copy, and if she signed the papers, it would be as if she had signed her own crucifixion papers. The innocent Diana or the smart Diana did not sign those papers. Her intuition sensed my father's fishy intentions, and she was proud of her marriage. At the time, in Brazil, a lawyer did not pressure a woman to sign her separation papers. As far as I understood, if the woman was innocent, honor was kept. This incident could be an entire book in itself.

CHAPTER 4

Rancho Aurora

By 1963, Daniela and my father had four children. David was born in May 1955, Fernando was born in November 1956, Lívia was born in September 1958, and Samantha was born in April 1960. By then, my father had eight children, counting the four of us: Ernesto, Eric, André Filho, and me, Katia. It seems that Daniela really wanted to have as many children as possible. The more kids, the more control she would have over him. Daniela eventually would become more demanding and, my father, who always implied that Daniela was his other half, would probably fulfill all her wants. This situation just made my mother's and our lives more difficult—even more difficult before the birth of Samantha, the latest addition.

My father and Daniela were living in a very small house when he purchased their first ranch, which became part of Rancho Aurora. They built a new house, perhaps in 1959 or the beginning of 1960, before Samantha's birth. This is destiny's irony. In our house, we knew that all the money my father made at his pharmacy went to pay for the purchase of two ranches and for the construction of Daniela's dream house.

The first part of the ranch was legally my father's property. Then Daniela asked him to buy the neighbor's ranch, which was for sale.

She probably manipulated him to make the purchase so he would give it to her as a gift. My father really did buy the other ranch. I guess he thought it would be an advantage for them to expand the property. The ranches together became a sort of a farm, yet he never planted enough crops to sell them in large quantities when Rancho Aurora became his residence.

After the expansion, my father planted lots of fruit trees, mostly for the family to consume. They also provided shade for many other small projects. My father had many employees. I remember that he planted a vegetable garden close to the house. Then he added a flower garden with roses and other flowers. One time, he told me at the pharmacy that he had planted a blue rose he found at a nursery in Santana. It was at the time an agricultural breakthrough; blue roses had never existed before.

The story was that a gardener in São Paulo read about an experiment in Europe, he tried the experiment, and it worked. Then nurseries around the country started to sell small planters already with the blue rose plant in them, and their special care was explained to blue rose lovers. After a few years, I remember seeing many residential gardens landscaped with different colors of roses, and the blue rose was always among them.

The land was fertile, and any tropical fruit would grow on his ranch: bananas, guavas, mangoes, oranges, pineapples, tangerines, and many others. My father planted several kinds of trees on his ranch. He planted many mango trees close to where he planned to build a house. After at least ten years, these mango trees provided lots of shade for the house and for the entrance as well. They could not plant apples, peaches, or pears. These fruit trees would not grow, as he lived in the northeast of the country. The summer was very hot. During summer, it rained a lot. Temperatures could rise to 100 degrees Fahrenheit or more. Brazil uses the metric system, so temperature is measured using Centigrade. So it would be 38 degrees Celsius or more.

The house was built on Daniela's part of the ranch. I believe that around 1959 or 1960, the value of the construction of a nice ranch house in a medium-size city in northeast Brazil, using the best wood and the best tiles, ceramic, and fixtures, was much more expensive than the land of the two ranches put together. The ranch, the brand-new house, and a new baby girl brought Daniela a lot of happiness while my mother and her children were living in a rental house. And the new baby, Samantha, looked like Daniela's father, who descended from Italians. (Daniela came from a very poor family descended from Africans and Italians, yet somehow, she was born white and with her father's features.) Her previous daughter, Lívia, looked more like Daniela's mother, Soraya, somehow dark-skinned.

Daniela spied on my mother's and father's lives while she lived in my parents' house for a year. She waited for the perfect time to jump for the gold. It was the big and quick jump of the cat. Daniela found a way to steal what didn't belong to her. It was like a spell. However, she never imagined any kind of revenge from God's angels.

They ran away from Monte Feliz in November 1953. By April 1960, she had a ranch that legally belonged to her—a nice ranch house and everything she could possibly imagine. After everything she managed to take from my mother, and having already lived with my father for ten years, she became worried that if he died, she would not inherit the other part of Rancho Aurora and her children would not inherit as much as his first children with Diana because she was not married to him. She just lived with him and had children with him.

I grew up always knowing that my father and Daniela betrayed my mother, my brothers, and me. When young children are betrayed, they never forget it because it's almost impossible for very young kids to just pretend. Children do not easily forget being tricked by others. When we are young, we are truthful to whatever we think or say, as during childhood, humans are truthful to themselves. Children don't like pretension, lies, or tricks. As adults, humans learn how to pretend or how to be sarcastic and ironic.

As early as five years old, I sensed when my mother was not happy, which actually was quite often at the time. The feeling of betrayal followed me like something sour from a fruit I did not want to taste. Once again, humiliation and betrayal followed my family around at home. For my mother, Ernesto, Eric, André Filho, and me, it was as if some people had really taken away what belonged to us and we couldn't do anything about it. This is the bitter taste of life.

How come my father did not think that we were suffering inside? His first children were just pretending to be happy kids. I guess at home we tried to live happily when we were not thinking about Rancho Aurora.

I am not implying that my family starved at home while my father lived in paradise with the other ones. Yet, by logic, his other family lived in a kingdom, with the king providing milk and honey for all of them and for others as well. My father would buy the cattle and the pigs, and Daniela would raise the chickens. So life for them was easier. My father did not give us an opportunity to have a ranch, and he never built a house for us.

When I was at the pharmacy while I was growing up, I would pay attention to my father's conversations with his employees or with my brothers, listening to see if he said he was planning to acquire something like a new icebox or TV. When I was a child, there were times that really affected me personally. For example, on my birthday, which was Saint John's Day, we had festivities. My father was never at my house. Nowadays, here in the United States when I hear fireworks, my mind goes back in time, and I have recollections of my childhood. I recall Saint John's Day.

Also, on Christmas Day, I have childhood recollections. I used to wake up very early, by 6:00 or 7:00 a.m., and look underneath my bed to see what Santa Claus left for me. As I grew up, I figured that my Santa Claus was actually my brother Eric, as he always asked my father in advance for some money to buy my Christmas present. On Christmas Eve, by 9:00 p.m., my mother used to say, "Go to sleep because if you don't sleep, Santa will not come." I knew that in other families' homes, fathers were Santa Claus; however, in my house, my brother Eric was our Santa Claus. Eric always thought about my Christmas gift, as he knew my father would be in his ranch with his other children.

This was life for the Oliveira Florencios. At home, it seemed that the angels had betrayed us or Christ was teaching us how to live without our father. Everything was upside down. Where were the angels for my family at home? Perhaps they could not do anything at this time.

I recall that by a certain age, perhaps twelve or thirteen years old, I started to think about life in other countries. At the time, in

1964, young Brazilians heard that France was and had been for a long time the country where rich families would send their children to get educated. We heard about the United States, but Steve Jobs and Bill Gates were not in the picture yet. No Apple computers, iPads or iPhones, or WordPerfect or Microsoft Word existed. We just read books, magazines, and newspapers to know what was going on in the world.

I recall that sometime in 1963 or 1964, my father bought a new TV for his house at Rancho Aurora. Soon, Ernesto asked him for a TV for us. If I recall correctly, after Ernesto saw the new TV in my father's and Daniela's ranch house, he asked my father to buy us a TV. Sometimes, my mother used to say, "If André had stayed with us, he wouldn't spend so much." We knew that two of everything, such as two TVs or two iceboxes, was too much for my father to pay for; however, my brothers and I were not the cause of this situation. The cause was life's circumstances.

Anyway, middle-class families could not afford to send their children abroad. Rich families could. At home, we had enough problems to think about. Going abroad was just a fantasy for me at the time. It was hard for me to overcome my parents' situation, which greatly affected my family members' lives.

Remembering my circumstances as a small five-year-old child, and also during my preadolescent days, I used to see my mother crying, and slowly, I began to understand why. All my life, as I recall, my father never asked me about my mother. He never really explained his relationship with her. We at home sensed and learned that they were two completely different beings. So I guess we never felt like asking him too many questions related to my mother and him. Actually, we avoided the subject. I believe that what my brothers and I wanted from my father as we were growing up was some kind of justice from him as he built the ranch house and also the gifts he gave to his other children.

As far as I remember, Ernesto was the courageous one who talked to my father and asked him something. When I was about eight or nine years old and Ernesto was sixteen to seventeen years old, he began to confront my father with questions. So we at home lived our lives not telling our friends too much about what was going on. The world out there—I mean, our friends—did not know much about our feelings toward our father. Our relatives, my aunt Janete and my uncle Joel, knew, as my uncle Joel was the one who brought us from Monte Feliz.

I never saw any of my brothers crying about missing our father or missing things at home. I never saw Eric or André confronting our father. As I said, by sixteen or seventeen, Ernesto slowly started to confront our father with questions. I don't know much about the questions he asked my father, yet he would tell my mother, Eric, André, and me about some of his conversations with my father.

The pharmacy was actually a meeting place for all of us. Sometimes on Sundays, we would go to church and then to his pharmacy. Then by lunchtime, we would go home. He would drive us to our home, and then he would go to Rancho Aurora. Rancho Aurora was his beloved home. My brothers, as boys and older than I was, used to see him every day, as they used to help and work in the pharmacy. My father wanted my brothers in the pharmacy every single day: half a day in school and then half a day in the pharmacy, which was his personal business.

If he wanted to talk to us about a family issue or any problem, he would tell us to come upstairs, and he would meet us there in private, where he kept a comfortable rocking chair to take naps. It was an old habit. Actually, in South America, people used to close their businesses during lunchtime, and they would go home to eat lunch and take a nap. Perhaps in small towns they still do. My father used to keep the pharmacy open, as he had employees. They used to bring their lunch with them, and then my father would make a simple schedule. Because the farm was not so far away from the pharmacy, some days, my father used to go to the farm to eat his lunch. On Mondays, quite frequently, Daniela prepared a big meal, and my father used to bring it to the pharmacy and share it with us, as Monday was a busy day when many country people came from their farms to shop in the city.

When I was about fourteen years old, my father closed his big Ipanema Pharmacy and kept just Sunshine Pharmacy, or Farmácia Brilho do Sol, open. By then, I had started to work as a cashier. He really wanted all his older children in the pharmacy as much as we could help him. Two of his employees had left, as Farmácia Brilho do Sol was somehow small compared to Ipanema. David and Fernando used to help him as well. Lívia, Samantha, and Eliana never helped at work, as they were much younger than I was.

David, Fernando, Samantha, and Lívia would go to the Presbyterian church on Sundays. This was at my father's request. My mother was Catholic before marrying my father; then after marrying my father, she started to attend the Presbyterian church. I believe they used to go to church with the boys, Ernesto, Eric, and André Junior, much before I was born. However, after the separation, my mother began attending church services at her old Catholic church, where my grandfather Leonardo Oliveira attended services with the rest of his family.

My father was a good man. I don't know how things turned out the way they did when Daniela interfered in his and my mother's lives. My father was the provider for all of us. However, time passed by, and we really felt that Rancho Aurora was a symbol of treason. There were times when just thinking of Rancho Aurora made me sad because my father lived there and lived his happiness as if his first children didn't exist. We only existed when we were in his pharmacy. That was very unfair.

He used to tell me that he sometimes invited pharmaceutical representatives to spend a weekend at the ranch. Some of them would bring their families. After hearing from him how he spent the weekend, I somehow used to feel jealous because I knew that his first children were not part of his social life at the ranch. For me, everything was so wrong, as my brothers and I were not part of his life at the ranch.

In this book, sometimes I am controversial. I should say that at home, my mother, my brothers, and I learned how to live our own happiness even if the wounds existed. The wounds were there. Perhaps it is life for some or for many. There are moments when we are happy; other times, we just pretend we are really happy. When we were in my father's pharmacy, we were happy, yet when he drove us home and then he drove to Rancho Aurora at the end of the day with his other children, it was as if we were entering a separate world that was our home, our own world. I guess my brothers and I just got used to coming home without my father. The next day, we would see him again.

At the time, as a preteen, I knew—or I wanted to believe—that one day in the future, the angels would come and they would bring us complete happiness. I did not know when because I was raised to believe that God brought us into this world to live happily. If that was the case, how could this be happening to me, my mother, and my brothers? When I was little, I believed in fairy tales. I would see myself in another country, with my own children running in a grassy yard with a garden, and looking up at the chimney, I would see smoke coming out because it was cold and it was Christmas. I did not know if I would have apple trees. Yet I could see in my vision lots of pine trees, and the trees would be covered with snow, and inside the house, there was a real Christmas tree. I guess this would be enough. And it really became a reality. It was a gift from God. And the gift from childhood illusions became real—very real.

Whatever my father and Daniela did, built, planted, and enjoyed on Rancho Aurora was, of course, for their own pleasure and for their children's pleasure. I did not live there. I recall times when on Sunday mornings, my father used to come to my house and take me to the ranch when we did not go to church, and he would tell my mother, "I am taking Katia to the ranch. I'll bring her later." My mother used to be preoccupied.

It was not so far to the ranch. I think it was about a twenty- to twenty-five-minute drive to reach Rancho Aurora. I remember seeing all sorts of fruit trees. I've never forgotten the fruit trees he had at the ranch: orange, mango, guava, papaya, and banana trees and other trees. Mostly bordering the driveway and the front gate, there were coconut trees and lots of flowers that enhanced Rancho Aurora's entrance. I remember the sound of the wind blowing through the leaves of the coconut trees, and I remember seeing the light of the sun touching the young green coconuts. For my father, Daniela, and their children, it was a real paradise, yet the paradise was not for me or my brothers or mother; if I actually said it was for us, I would be pretending. I would be lying to myself.

Sometimes, in conversation with friends or colleagues at school, I used to say that my father had a pharmacy and a beautiful ranch, yet inside, I felt sad because Rancho Aurora, the ranch where my father lived, was not my home; it was not my ranch. It was my father's home. It was actually the home of Daniela, his companion—the one he lived with until he died, even if he betrayed her. It belonged to Daniela and their children. It was their home sweet home.

CHAPTER 5

The Flight of the Eagles

By 1963 or 1964, Daniela began pressing my father to ask my mother for a divorce, as she wanted to marry him, knowing that if my father died, my mother legally would inherit 50 percent of his part of Rancho Aurora, and then his first children, the Oliveira Florencios, would inherit a higher percentage of the other 50 percent of the ranch because we were the children of a legally married couple. Daniela tried to take everything that she could possibly take, like an eagle ready to kill its pray. She probably wanted to take as much as she could in order to secure her and her children's future.

For us, the Oliveira Florencios, if Daniela married my father and he passed away, she would have won the war. Probably she would find a way to take as much as she could for her children as a married woman. However, this never happened. In this case, my mother was really smart for not conceding the divorce. My father never prepared a will. He never had a will because he considered himself young and healthy. He never smoked, and he never drank. He told us, his children, that he would die very old. I guess he implied that he would live until one hundred years old or he would outlive my mother and perhaps his companion, Daniela. The only drinks he liked were

Coca-Cola and Guarana, which is a sweet and light drink like Sprite yet much better.

If Daniela had the opportunity to marry my father, it would be a disaster. She probably would be in charge of the division of his assets. Years before my father passed away, when I was nine, ten, and eleven years old, Daniela divided a small part of her land, and she was selling property lots. I never asked my brothers or my father any questions, yet I really felt that it was unfair, as he was paying for the advertising; besides, she had gotten the gift years ago and probably paid for the division of the lots, construction workers, lights on the new streets, the pavement, et cetera. Now, she was making money on the land. More and more, I felt that too much had been taken from us, the Oliveira Florencios, and my father should be the one to provide us with what he provided mostly to Daniela, as her children were still small. She was building their nest.

Sometime during 1963 or 1964, I remember listening many times to someone advertising the lots on the radio: "Soup, soup, soup! Who doesn't like a good soup? Buy from Loteamento Irmãos Santana. The price is right; the price is good! You can have your house ready to move in before Christmas! Come and see for yourself." The name of the lots translates in English as "Santana Brothers' Lots." An address and a telephone number were provided. Rancho Aurora had no telephone number at that time. People could call Ipanema Pharmacy and talk to André Florencio, or anyone could drive to the ranch, as the address was provided. If needed, my father would drive anyone interested in the purchase of a property lot to Rancho Aurora.

The lots didn't even have the name *Florencio*, our father's family name. Daniela didn't want anything carrying the name *Florencio*, as she was not married to my father. She didn't want anything to sound as if it could belong to us, the Oliveira Florencios, so the lots were called Loteamento Irmãos Santana. My father would even tell us, "Daniela is selling Loteamento Irmãos Santana." He told us to listen to the radio and check the largest newspaper in the state at the time, *A Tarde*. In English, this means *"The Afternoon."* So he was spending money to advertise the sale of her lots in many ways. I always tried to check the newspaper for the advertisement about Santana Brothers' Lots. The marketing at the time was good for buying and selling.

I vividly remember asking myself, *Where are* our *lots?* I didn't confront my father, as I did not have the courage and I was just nine, ten, or eleven years old.

These lots were being sold in 1963, 1964, and 1965. I began listening to the radio announcements about the sale of Santana Brothers' Lots. These incidents happened five, six, and seven years before my father's death. After he passed away, Daniela somehow survived well. She had other lots to sell, as the land was immense. She also raised many animals—cows, pigs, and chickens—and I know that Daniela had a good reserve in the bank.

After Ernesto and Amanda left Santana to start their new lives, Daniela never called Ernesto to ask for help with money or other needs. That's why I knew that Daniela was doing well. She had her animals, and she had lots of fruit trees, so she sold animals and fruit. The fruit trees provided fruit she probably sold whenever it was in season. So it's evident that she prepared herself well for unexpected situations.

Lívia and David did not attend college, yet they managed to work after high school. Later in life, Lívia got married and worked as an administrative assistant in a local school. David got married as well and bought a big truck and worked for himself selling soda and beer in local restaurants. Samantha and Eliana pursued college educations at the state university, which had been transferred from downtown to the campus very close to Rancho Aurora. As the state university moved to the location very close to the ranch, Samantha and Eliana had the advantage of taking classes close to home. Samantha pursued a master's degree in education, and later, she also received a PhD in pedagogy. She was lucky, as state universities in medium-size cities and in the capital do not charge fees for classes. Anybody can get a degree without having debts or loans at the end of the program. Students just have to pass an entrance test. When the state faculty was located downtown, I took classes there during my first year of college.

All of Daniela's children got married or lived with someone. She was happy, as after a few years, they all were independent. Rancho Aurora was really a paradise for Daniela and her children as much as it was for my father. He was the one who told me how much he loved Rancho Aurora. It was peaceful to rest under mango trees in a hammock, listening to the birds at his own place, after a day's work.

Fernando decided to leave Santana to pursue a technical education in Salvador, the capital of Bahia. He managed to work and to go to school. As soon as he finished his technical preparation, he opened his own business.

Ernesto kept the pharmacy for almost two years. After a year of planning and arranging things in the pharmacy, by December 1971, he and Amanda got married on a beautiful Saturday morning. The sun shined, and we all, the Oliveira Florencios, the Santana Florencios, and Amanda's family, the Rodrigueses, enjoyed the party, as did many friends, mostly Amanda's since Petrolina was her hometown. We all enjoyed Amanda and Ernesto's spectacular wedding. It was unforgettable. They were married in the beautiful white cathedral.

After their wedding and honeymoon, Ernesto and Amanda came to Santana to live for some time, as Ernesto was planning to get a job as an agricultural engineer, and actually, after a year and a half working at Farmácia Brilho do Sol, they left for another city close to Salvador, which was much better for shopping and entertainment. Ernesto finally found a job working with farmers doing agricultural projects.

Perhaps a week after my father passed away, a man wearing a hat began appearing at the pharmacy every Saturday morning. He was the country girl's father. She had a little boy. She needed Ernesto's help to take care of the kid. So the old man would come talk to Ernesto about the little boy and take some money as well. What I came to know about the farmer coming to the pharmacy was that he was my father's employee and the grandfather of my father's son with the man's daughter. I guess the romance began when my father probably was taking his farm employees to their homes in the late afternoon after the day's work. Probably the family served coffee and cake, as it is the habit with visitors. And then from there, my father began a romance with the farmer's daughter.

As I said previously, I knew something had been going on with my father and a countrywoman before he passed away; however, I came to know the real story between my father and this country girl after the funeral and after seeing the man in the hat standing up at the counter for an hour or so on Saturday mornings, waiting to talk to Ernesto. It was one more responsibility for Ernesto to figure out, as so many unexpected things appeared after my father's passing.

After my father died, Ernesto realized that he had to take my father's place managing the pharmacy and to find a solution for the problems my father had left behind, and he knew he was the one to really take his place in the business, at least for the time being. When my father died, I was just sixteen years old, and I did not know what would happen to our family and to Daniela and her children as well. During the affair, Ernesto was engaged to Amanda and, as said, would eventually get married and leave our house. He planned to get an agricultural engineering job, but that could not support so many people. I guess after my father's death, Amanda became preoccupied by the situation.

As we walked to give my father a last good-bye, actually a farewell, I was told that Iracema, the little boy's mother, my father's last lover, was in despair. How would she support her son? He left nothing in writing to tell us about this person and their son. As I was just sixteen, I somehow sensed that everybody in the family had to swim almost alone. I knew that we had to swim to survive; otherwise, we would sink. That was what Iracema had to do. She was a countrywoman living with her parents, I believe with no education at all. I just couldn't imagine how a young woman living on a farm with her poor parents and a young child would survive. She would probably eventually get married to a countryman, and then she would have to pray a lot for God to give her strength to raise her child. Now, her old father, one of my father's employees, had his hands full.

Daniela, alone with her young children, her sick mother, and an old aunt to support at Rancho Aurora, had to continue raising her animals, and she had to sell some land, as the farm would provide her money with which to live and educate her children. At least she was a smart woman, or more than that, she learned how to manipulate my father very well.

Only after his passing did I come to know that half the huge ranch legally belonged to Daniela. As a result, my brothers and I could not do anything with my father's legal part of Rancho Aurora when he died.

I was just sixteen years old, and the other children were so young. The best solution was to leave everything the way it was. Daniela would continue to live in her house and in her ranch, and she could take care of or just watch the other part of the land because it was in her own interest, as her children would inherit something from the land.

My father did not leave any will. We knew that someday we would get a lawyer to resolve our situation, yet my brother Ernesto realized that he could not immediately sell the pharmacy. He had to contact a lawyer, and he needed to stay with the business for some time to figure out how to deal with the situation, so all of us could not even think about inheritances. Ernesto knew that Rancho Aurora was actually two ranches put together yet with separate papers. So the part that belonged to my father would be divided. Fifty percent would belong to my mother as his legal wife, and the other 50 percent would be subdivided among nine children. The little boy would eventually get something someday. So Rancho Aurora's papers stayed the same for almost thirty-five years. Eventually, it would be subdivided, according the law.

Sorrow, anguish, and fear followed Daniela for days after my father's passing. David and Fernando were just fifteen and fourteen years old. Lívia, Samantha, and Eliana were respectively ten, nine, and six years old. My father had legally left Daniela part of Rancho Aurora, which was and still is a huge ranch with many fruit trees that he and Daniela planted over the years, plus some cattle, pigs, and other farm animals. Daniela would continue raising her cattle, pigs, and chickens. She had at least a couple of cows for milk. My father and Daniela had lots of employees to take care of the ranch. But after he passed away, Daniela had to ask most of the ranch workers to leave because it would be impossible for her to pay the people without his help.

Days, weeks, months, and years that followed my father's death were difficult for all of us. Despite what my father left for Daniela, she was scared of the future. She was not sure she could survive without him. I guess Daniela had so much fear because her oldest son, David, was just fifteen years old and Farmácia Brilho do Sol would not be enough to support so many people. Daniela had under her care her sick mother and an old aunt, and she knew that Ernesto had to take care of my mother and myself until I eventually finished high school, and then I had to attend a state college. Days after my father's passing, Eric and André Junior left Santana for Salvador again to try to pass the college entrance test. They were about to start college, but that depended on some entrance tests. The results: Eric passed the tests; however, André did not.

After five harsh and difficult years, Eric graduated as an architect from Federal University based in Salvador. Years later, Eric married Susana. Soon after getting his college entrance test results, André got a good job, and years later, he married Camilla. Both managed to spend a year in London. I was happy he learned English enough to study system analysis. After coming back from England, he would have a boost toward getting a job, which he needed to support his new family.

Following my father's death, I remember seeing my mother crying, and then I decided to ask her what kind of feelings she had felt for him when, sixteen years before, he had left her pregnant with me. Now he was dead; however, she had loved him all her life. When I asked her this question, even when I was younger, she would answer me, "For your father I have love and hate." And I would think, *Isn't it strange?* She did not hate him completely. That's why she never accepted legally separating from him.

She was born on a farm before the Second World War. Her mother died when she was just seven years old, and I think she had dyslexia. I always used to notice that she had a hard time reading well and clearly. Always, she staggered. So she needed some kind of emotional support, and deep inside, the marriage was an honor for her, even when he left her and lived with Daniela until he died. Nowadays, working with schoolchildren, I've learned how to recognize dyslexia. It causes frustration when trying to read in front of others. The story of my mother is really the story of a woman on a cross.

She had so many stories; the saddest was from when my father was about to leave her one day in November 1953. Out of nowhere, he looked at her and said, "Saturday, three days from now, I will be leaving Monte Feliz. I am going to Santana because I want to open a new pharmacy, and then I need time to make money and get settled. You and the kids will come later. I need to find a place for me and

Daniela to live. She will help me in the pharmacy, as she has acquired good experience in the pharmacy here in Monte Feliz. Then I will come back, or perhaps I will ask your brother to bring you and the kids to Santana, but not yet. I don't know when. You have to be patient. I can't live with you anymore. I can't live in peace with you. Hold yourself here. I have to go. Daniela will help me. We know that she comes from a poor family; actually, she does not even have a father, yet she can read and write, and she is smart. We know where she is coming from. However, she will be my right arm." These words were like a shot to my mother's heart. She knew that her life with my father was over. She just believed in God and felt that he would not leave her alone. How cold were those words. It's hard to believe how she managed to listen to him so simply saying that he was leaving in just three days.

My mother immediately felt depressed and fearful. She just cried, asking him, "How am I going to live alone with the kids until you come to take us to Santana?" She continued, saying that she could not believe what she just heard. Recalling the event for me, she said, "I told him that I did not have inheritances and that I was expecting a child and he knew about it." Then she told me that my father replied, "I will come here once a month to leave the money for the house expenses. Talk to your brother. I know he is living in Santana as well. He comes here almost every month to see your father. We will work on a plan together for you and the kids."

At the time, my mother just could not believe what was happening. *Why did he plan this secret escape with Daniela and not even tell his two oldest sons? They will fall into a depression as well,* she thought. *This is betraying his own children.* She thought that at least he would take her and the kids with him. Then Daniela would follow him; perhaps Daniela could take a bus to Santana. That was her thought. She was so naïve.

When my mother would tell me this story, I used to feel so much compassion for her innocence. I really thought that she had some intuition, yet she couldn't do anything. It was as if the spell was done. And I could not think about anything else; I would just listen to her stories. Inside, I believed some anguish and feelings of deep compassion would torture me. I have heard in Brazil, and even here in the United

States on a radio station in Georgia, that karma will follow the traitor. Someday, this traitor would suffer; actually, she would pay. I mean, my mother implied that someday Daniela would pay. Not with money; probably with divine punishment. For some reason, she thought that some kind of spell was taking my father away.

I believe that Daniela was already living in fear, as the community was composed of many Catholic Italians and nobody in town would accept their living together, and my father knew that. Both knew they had to leave. The town of Monte Feliz was very small. Leaving his family with an employee who had actually lived in our house before I was born was really treason. How could Daniela do this? And why did she do this?

The reality was that Daniela had been paying attention to my mother's life— her personality, her ways, and her naïveté—and quietly, she studied the family's habits and problems; actually, she paid attention to everything. Of course, she realized that taking my father away from my mother was just a matter of time. The devil knows how to play dirty. Probably she thought, *I will get André when the time comes.* That was her evil intention.

Daniela had lived in our house, as my father told my mother two years before the getaway, when Daniela did not have a place to live. She did not have a father. She and her mother were living with her aunt, who had a hostel that they called "Pensão." My mother, feeling compassion following my father's words, had accepted the woman who eventually would betray her.

My mother almost lost her mind, as I was told by my brother Ernesto and my aunt Janete. She cried every day. My aunt Janete at the time was still living in Monte Feliz, as was my mother's father, my grandfather Leonardo Oliveira, with his second wife. My mother's mother had died when she was very young. Also, my grandmother Marilia, my father's mother, was my mother's neighbor; she lived just three houses down the street. After my father left, my aunt Janete and my grandmother Marilia constantly came to help and to provide emotional support as well. They knew that my mother needed so much help with her kids and she needed to talk to try to release her fears and sorrows. A woman alone with three young children and expecting a new one was left alone without a plan.

What happened was that Daniela had secretly planned everything with my father. My mother's life went upside down. At the time, I was not born yet. Many times as a teenager and later in my life, I wondered how my mother did cope with his absence. My grandfather, my father's father, had passed away when my oldest brother was still a baby. So my grandmother Marilia had been a widow for at least seven years. In reality, they needed each other for support.

Can you imagine a woman living in a small town in rural Brazil in 1953 being told, by surprise, by her husband that he is leaving with another woman? What an escape! It sounds as if Daniela planned the perfect escape. I know that she felt she was not safe in Monte Feliz. My mother told me that at the time, if a single woman secretly dated a married man—and more, if the couple had children—then someone from the wife's family, like a brother, a cousin, or even a friend, could secretly talk to the young woman and give her a warning to leave the town and never come back, as she was becoming a threat for the community.

God shows his mercy when we believe in him. The Catholic people in Brazil say that God sometimes is late, yet he shows up sooner or later. I guess he held my mother, Diana, from insanity, as I don't know how she survived for eighteen months without my father and how my brothers received the surprise. Ernesto and Eric must have cried for days, weeks, and months.

My mother told me that the day I was born, he was not there. He was still in Santana. Someone in the family sent him a telegram announcing my birth. A doctor in town came to perform the delivery. I guess my father drove perhaps ten or more hours to Monte Feliz to see his little girl. It seems that he was expecting a boy. Well, my mother really prayed to have a daughter, and her prayers were answered.

I feel that while my mother was pregnant with me, her depression followed her, and I believe that the feelings of abandonment and betrayal she felt during pregnancy really affected me. When I was about five years old, I would find her crying, and I would ask her if she had a headache, and she would say, "It's nothing," because she could not explain her problems to a five-year-old.

I have early recollections of our first old house. I recall seeing a guava tree and a papaya tree in the yard, which provided some shade and fruits for us. One day, I saw a young girl through the fence that separated our yards. Her name was Amalia. We became friends. Soon, her mother asked my mother to let me come to the big house every Sunday to play with the little girl. I remember that I was invited to eat lunch with them as well. I can't forget the smell of the cilantro and the taste of the food. And then the meal was followed by a coconut cake. The aroma from the oven would arrive in the dining room long before the cake. Then the sweet coconut cake would be on the table.

I remember the entrance of the beautiful house. There was a huge yard. Amalia's father had planted some imperial palm trees along the entrance, and they had the most beautiful garden in the world in the eyes of a five-year-old. It was really beautiful. Today, when I recall living in our first house on Sunshine Street during my childhood, I even recall the smell of our neighbor Amalia's garden, which had so many different plants and flowers. Before I met this family, I believe they knew that my father did not live with us. My father used to drive my brothers back from the pharmacy every day. And I guess the neighbors could see and hear my father's small truck dropping off my brothers.

My mother told Senhora Teresa our story. Perhaps knowing the story, Senhora Teresa began to invite me almost every Sunday to have lunch and to play with Amalia. My mother had probably told Senhora Teresa that my father lived on a nice farm with a nice ranch house. So, as a young child, I probably felt so pleased to have a friend whose parents enjoyed having me in the house and who treated me like their own daughter. Psychologically, this admiration for my friend's house compensated for my lack of a father and what he could have provided for us.

My brothers and I were my father's first children. We did not have a nice house as our neighbor. Rancho Aurora and the ranch house were symbols of betrayal. My admiration for my neighbor's house was my soul and spirit trying to fill the emptiness that the separation left behind. When I was a five- or six-year-old, my mother, perhaps because of her own feelings of abandonment, used to tell me repeatedly that I was somehow rejected.

Growing up, I slowly came to understand that my father did not reject me, yet there were circumstances that greatly affected me.

Psychologically, childhood memories stay inside us. It took time—a long time—for me to understand what really happened. A man feeling empty or unfulfilled finds another woman and feels a connection, so he just jumps in. Then later, sometimes he repeats the sin. Perhaps my father needed some kind of therapy at the time. I believe my father was not completely fulfilled as a man or perhaps a human being because before his death, he had a new relationship out of nowhere, and then he conceived a son.

I met my half-brother in December 2012. He was the little boy I've mentioned many times in this book. By the grace of God, this man managed to survive. He grew up seeing and experiencing so much poverty. One day, his mother started to take him to a Christian church, where God found a way to save him. Now, my youngest half-brother is a pastor at a large Christian church in Brazil. He firmly believes that God saved him.

Whoever reads this book, please never abandon a child. The suffering produces marks that stay forever. The only way to live happily is to believe that someday—perhaps today or tomorrow—God's angels will come. If someone makes a child suffer, someday, the angels could come and act in revenge. I never wanted any kind of revenge because God is the one who sees what some of us are doing on the planet on which we live: Earth.

My mother told me that after my father left her and her children, she believed that the only way for her to combat all the suffering and humiliation she went through was by praying for God and Christ's mother to keep her from falling. Being Catholic, perhaps she was told by her father or her relatives that the ones who made her suffer probably would have their day of judgment. It was not that she would use her hands for vengeance; instead, the angels would come act on her behalf.

Life is like the waves of the sea, which come and go. Some days, the ocean is blue; some days, the ocean is tumultuous, raging, and dark. A sunny and beautiful day will always come. Just know that tomorrow is another day.

CHAPTER 6

The Good Samaritan

My mother never got over the separation, so not divorcing him was her revenge. Even if in her mind the Santana Florencios had taken my father away from us, or he chose his own path as he ran away with Daniela, my mother was still married to him. My father always implied that Daniela had become his companion and best friend. However, after twelve or thirteen years, everything changed because he betrayed her the same way he betrayed my mother.

Daniela and my father had their happy days. By April 1960, Daniela gave birth to a baby girl. My father took Ernesto, Eric, and André to meet their new half-sister. At the time, I was almost six years old. I recall that my brother Ernesto had a conversation with my mother, and he mentioned that the baby was white and cute and it seemed she was very special to Daniela and my father. Ernesto mentioned that she did not look like her sister, Lívia, who resembled Daniela's mother and relatives.

My mother told Ernesto that she felt that my father was going to be too busy with the new addition. Then she started to recall the past, asking Ernesto if he remembered when I was born. Ernesto answered, "Yes, Mom. It was Saint John's Day." He even remembered that our grandmother Marilia, who was our neighbor, had brought some firewood the day before to set up the bonfire, as my mother was already tired and expecting her child, who would be me, at any time.

After the conversation with Ernesto, my mother told me that she was planning to visit my uncle Joel and his wife, my aunt Laura, the next day. Her brother had helped her emotionally, and also, he was the one who brought us to Santana, the new city in which we were living.

* * *

The next morning, we went to visit my uncle Joel and my aunt Laura. There, my mother told my uncle about the new baby, crying because she was jealous of my father's new daughter and because she remembered when I was born, he was far away, already living with his companion, Daniela, in this city. She felt that my father did not know what she went through without him. My uncle and aunt comforted her; however, my uncle became upset. He knew that he could not change anything. He just told my mother to be strong and have faith in God. He reminded her that, somehow, she was now close to my father and that she was not as alone as she was five years ago when he brought us from Monte Feliz, as my uncle and aunt were there for her. They had moved to Santana a year before my father had set up a residence with Daniela. At the time, the city was growing; many people had come from small towns to start their businesses, as they knew they would prosper there.

My mother and my uncle continued to talk, and I remember my uncle telling my mother that he had kept the telegram she sent to him when my father left her. My uncle told my mother that when he first read the telegram, immediately, he couldn't believe the words he read. Recalling the day my father surprised her, my mother told my uncle that at that time, he was the only person who could talk to my father on her behalf.

My uncle told my mother that he would be by her side and that he knew she could not work since she had the kids. My mother agreed; she told her brother that she could not do anything unless she had a ranch or a farm where she could raise animals, as Daniela and my father were doing on their ranch. At that time, most single women would graduate to become teachers, and married ones would stay home with their kids. That was the happiness of a married couple.

* * *

Three years after Samantha's birth, by June 1963, Daniela surprised my father, telling him that she was pregnant again. Nine months later, in March 1964, another baby girl, Eliana, was born. By this time, my father had nine children. I recall that my father took me to meet the new baby, Eliana. She looked like the Italians who live along the Mediterranean. She was cute with dark hair, and her skin was sun-kissed—or, as we say in Portuguese, *pele morena*.

After Eliana was born, my father decided to open two small pharmacies in two small cities outside of Santana. The first pharmacy was located in a city called Nossa Senhora da Conceição, which in English translates to "Our Lady of Conception," that is about thirty-five miles from Santana, and the second one was located in another beautiful small town called Coração de Maria, which translates in English as "Heart of Mary." From the first city, it took just thirty minutes to reach the second, with perhaps fifteen miles between them.

After opening these two pharmacies, my father used to take me with him once a week, and while he drove, we would talk. Many times, David and Fernando went with us as well. At that time, the roads were safe, and I remember seeing hitchhikers walking along the road. Sometimes, my father would stop to give one or two hitchhikers a ride. However, he would charge a small amount; then he would give me the money, or if David and Fernando were with us, we would split the amount. I really liked to go to these cities; I went mostly when I was on vacation or when I did not have any homework for the next school day.

Coração de Maria was a beautiful small town. The central garden was well landscaped with lots of trees, which provided shade for the small park and for the pathways where people would stroll mostly in the afternoon. We always left Santana after lunch for the trip. By the time my father was ready to return to Santana, it would be around 5:00 p.m. I remember seeing the light of the setting sun passing through the foliage. These were relaxing days.

My father had two of his old employees manage these two pharmacies. He taught them how to make sales and how to manage his businesses. When he opened the pharmacy in Nossa Senhora da Conceição, an Afro-Brazilian man talked to him about the possibility of getting a job for his daughter. This man told my father that his wife had died and his daughter, Sabrina, was in her twenties and she really needed to work. I mentioned Sabrina briefly in chapter II. I am almost sure that Sabrina didn't have a middle school or high school education, yet per my father's conversation, Sabrina was very smart.

My father told Daniela that he wanted to employ Sabrina at his Ipanema Pharmacy, but to do that, she would need a place to live, so he had decided to bring her to live in their ranch house. Daniela accepted my father's idea. I don't know if Daniela liked the plan, but when my father decided to do something, it was almost impossible for someone in the family to say no.

When Sabrina came to live in the ranch house, every morning, my father and Sabrina would come to Ipanema Pharmacy in his car together, and then they would return together at night. Sometimes, David and Fernando would join them. For some reason, after Sabrina started working in the pharmacy, my brothers and I began to have suspicions toward the young Afro-Brazilian.

I guess less than a year after Sabrina started the job at the pharmacy, my father told me that Sabrina mentioned to him she wanted to go back to school. There was a public school that offered night classes. I came to know that by coincidence—or by no coincidence at all—she began attending the same private school I was attending. My classes took place in the afternoon, and she took classes at night after work. I don't know what agreement my father and Sabrina had.

Many times, I thought that I really did not know my father too well. After two years of working in the pharmacy and attending classes at night, one day, Sabrina had on a diamond ring in exactly the same design as the one my father had given me a few months before. I was curious, and I asked her where she had got the ring. She answered that she did not know because it was a gift from my father. I looked at her almost in disbelief.

At home, I mentioned this to Ernesto, Eric, and André. They told me that they also had seen Sabrina with a new ring on her right finger. We talked about it, and we thought that if my father was a good Samaritan, as he had appeared to be, it was fine that he had brought Sabrina to live in his ranch house; however, buying a diamond ring for an employee—when he had three other daughters and so many responsibilities with so many people—was a difficult-to-understand approach. After that, at home, we became suspicious. Was this one more repetition of his sin?

* * *

When my father passed away, Sabrina was still living at the ranch house. After his death, she continued working at the pharmacy with Ernesto for about a year. Then she left. Sometimes, we talked, and one day, she revealed to me that, three years before my father's death, when he had bought a new farm to raise cattle, he confided in her that he was having a romance with the daughter of one of his employees. If she knew, he probably had told her about it. I mentioned this to my brothers, and we figured that she had become, besides his protégé, his true confidant and friend. So many revelations came out after my father's death that, at the time, I did not stop to think too much about how enigmatic my father was, because after all, he had been a good man to people who knew him—people who became his customers at his pharmacy.

My mother told me that when she married my father, they both attended the Presbyterian church because my grandfather, my father's father, was Presbyterian. She said that my father was a trustful young man, the son of a middle-class, working father who was respected in the town of Monte Feliz, where they were born, and that both my mother's and my father's families had lived there for many years. It seems that my mother did not really convert to Presbyterianism. Perhaps she did at the time, but when my father left her, she talked to her father, my grandfather Leonardo, about her decision to start attending the Catholic church again, and forever, she would consider herself Catholic by faith.

I don't remember my father attending the church while he was alive. Perhaps he felt that it was too difficult to attend church while having two families, or perhaps the church pastor had talked to him about his situation. Sometimes while resting in his rocking chair at his pharmacy, I remember seeing my father reading the Bible, and I suppose he enjoyed the stories about good Samaritans. And then, he came to be a very good one.

CHAPTER 7

The Fall of the Bedroom Wall

Every June, the celebration of Saint John was exciting. Each year, we built a bonfire in front of our house, and we bought fireworks for the night celebration, and our neighbors, especially the children, would come to our house to eat corn muffins, cakes, boiled peanuts, and corn cooked on a stick on the bonfire as my mother prepared the table for us and our neighbors and friends.

We bought oranges to peel and eat by the fire; also, we used to make fresh orange juice. If my father had harvested corn and oranges on the farm, then he would bring them to us. But eventually, he did not join us for the two-night celebration: June 23 and 24. June 24 was the day Saint John was born. We used to pray for Saint John to hold off rain for two consecutive days: June 23 and 24. I got used to celebrating Saint John's Day without my father. My mother, brothers, and I just enjoyed the festival with our neighbors and friends. I did not know what was happening at my father's ranch house; however, my brothers and I would see him in the pharmacy on those two days.

Besides the oranges and the corn, we had to have peanuts. It was an unforgettable part of the celebration. We had to buy the peanuts the morning of June 23 or the day before in the open market downtown because it took almost all day to boil them. Also, every year, my mother would plan in advance to have a seamstress sew a country dress for me. The dress always was very colorful and funny. It had to resemble a farm girl's dress. Sometimes, girls and boys used to wear straw hats for Saint John's Day as well.

Also, on June 27 and June 28, many houses in our neighborhood had celebrations. On June 28, the widows celebrated their special day. They made a bonfire to celebrate Saint Peter's Day, as it was called the Day of the Widows. Perhaps I can compare Saint John's Day to Thanksgiving Day in the United States, as winter in Brazil happens during the months of June, July, and August.

That's when corn and other winter produce are harvested, mostly in the north and northeast parts of the country. However, for me, Saint John's Day was much more exciting than any other day of the year, as it was a festival all over the country, mostly celebrated in small towns and on farms, and people would make huge bonfires and organize Saint John's dances.

For some reason, I really recall the celebrations we had in an old house we lived in for about three years. The last time we celebrated Saint John's in this place was in June 1965. This old house must have been built in the second or third decade of the twentieth century because the house did not have a nice ceiling or even a nice architecture, unlike previous houses we had lived in. Also, the restroom was outside, not connected to the house, like at my father's ranch house. It really was a very old house. We did not know if it was made of brick or adobe. At night, after locking the door with a huge antique key, we had to put a heavy iron bar across the front door to safely secure it. After living in Monte Feliz, we lived in three houses, including this one, before my father finally bought a house for us.

The amazing and scary story in this chapter is about to begin. Normally during winter, we had rain, sometimes for two consecutive days. During the winter of 1965, the city hall decided to open a new street exactly where we were living. Two of our neighbors, a widow and her daughter, who lived right next to our house had to sell their place, as the city hall had somehow forced them to move away. The house was sold for the new street-building project. We did not know too much about this new street. This was a surprise for us.

The rain began to pour in June, and it kept raining in July as well. Then, on an early morning, my mother and I were sleeping before she walked up to my bed, woke me up, and said, "Katia, Katia, get up. Look at what just happened; the bedroom wall just fell." Then she yelled to my brothers, who were sleeping in the other bedroom, and she began to cry, scared and in disbelief of what she was seeing. Part of the wall had just fallen on our beds, and we could see the street and the mud from the rain that had accumulated on the ground. That's when we realized the house was made of adobe. It was soft and unsecured, like houses from the nineteenth century.

My mother told Ernesto, Eric, and André to get dressed, as we could see some neighbors were coming to see what had happened. We changed clothes as fast as we could. We felt sort of humiliated, as deep inside, we realized our father's negligence.

By then, it was around seven on Saturday morning. Ernesto ran to the pharmacy, hoping to see my father, as sometimes, he liked to open the pharmacy before 8:00 a.m. By the time Ernesto reached the pharmacy, my father was already there. I think he was shocked to see Ernesto so early, as he was not expecting him or he had not asked him to be there by that time. Ernesto explained what happened.

My father talked to Sabrina, and then he drove Ernesto to our house. It was not so far from the pharmacy.

When he got out of the car and walked close to the house, he could not believe what he saw. I never saw my father so pale; he really was shocked by what he was seeing. Then he took Ernesto with him and drove off to bring a carpenter, someone who actually had worked at his ranch house during the construction. My father returned with Ernesto and Senhor José, who brought a large piece of plywood to temporarily replace the wall that had fallen. It could not take the place of the entire bedroom wall; however, it needed to be blocked immediately for safety.

My father told Ernesto, Eric, André, and me to calm down and said that he would find a place for us. I don't remember seeing him talking to my mother. He told us that he had to call some people he knew in order to perhaps resolve the purchase of a house.

My Father and Me

Because our city was safe at the time, we spent about a week still living in this old house until Ernesto told us our father had managed to do some business with an old friend. This man was selling a house that his wife had inherited. The house was located in an area far away from the house we were living in and the pharmacy in downtown Santana. So finally, my mother, my brothers, and I quickly moved. We all were happy to be in another house. It was not a new house; however, it was much better than the one we had been living in, and it was our own house. The angels took a long time to intercede for us. Yet finally, it happened. I think that Daniela was not happy at all about this unexpected situation, as my father now had to work to pay for the new property.

This house had a front yard—actually, a small and simple garden. Soon, my father sent some people over to do some yard work. My mother noticed that whoever lived there before had planted daisies and herbs; she saw lots of mint leaves. These small plants were mixed in with the grass. The garden reminded us of our grandmother Marilia. She always kept all sorts of herbs in the backyard of her small house: mint, basil, chamomile, and other things.

We were happy to be in our own house. We had to take a bus to go to my father's pharmacy, as the house was quite a distance from the pharmacy. Yet, as always, while at the pharmacy, my father would bring us back home at the end of the day and also for lunch. By this time, Ernesto and Eric were driving, and they would sometimes drive home for lunch. Then we would go back to the pharmacy or to school when we had afternoon school sessions.

By then, my grandmother was living in Santana—actually, on the same street as my father's first pharmacy, Ipanema Pharmacy. My father had sold my grandmother's house in Monte Feliz a year after we left that city, and then he bought a small house in Santana for his mother because when my father left Monte Feliz with Daniela in November 1953, my grandmother cried a lot. She had just two children, and my father was the one who took care of her. Her husband had died in 1945, during the Second World War, before Ernesto was born in 1946.

My mother told me that when she got married, she and my father lived in my grandmother's house for a few months. She remembered

49

that my grandmother used to sew her own dresses by hand, and she mentioned that she smelled like mint leaves because she always kept herbs in the pockets of her dresses. When my grandmother moved to Santana, she again planted her preferred herbs: mint, basil, and chamomile. I vividly remember my grandmother smelling those mint leaves she kept in her pocket. Perhaps it was a common habit for people there at that time. My grandmother made all sorts of teas for sore throats and headaches; many times, I recall drinking chamomile tea, as she told me it would help me relax and sleep well.

Anyway, this began a new phase in my mother's, my brothers', and my life. Slowly, we adjusted to the new house and the new neighbors. Also, we got used to the distance from the new house to my father's pharmacy. With time, we realized it was just a thirty-minute drive from the house to downtown Santana. The house was located on an avenue where trees were planted between the two streets that made up Brasilia Avenue, which is the name of Brazil's capital. Note that in Portuguese, the word *Brazil* is written as *Brasil*, with an *s*. In English, Brazil is written with a *z*.

We lived in this house for many years, until after my father's death. We moved with Ernesto and Amanda to a small town, where Ernesto worked as an agricultural engineer. After my father's death and after I graduated from high school, it was time for our family to go on with our journeys. My father was gone. We just had to live. And we did.

CHAPTER 8

The Roller Coaster of the Mind

Since my childhood, I had been told that people born with the astrological sign of Cancer, which is the fourth Zodiac sign and a water sign, are dreamers who are sensitive to people's emotions, caring, and compassionate and believers in a bright and successful future for themselves. I am one of them, and my father was one of these dreamers as well. He was born in July, part of which belongs to the astrological sign of Cancer.

I vividly recall my father being caring, compassionate, and very sensitive to people's emotions. This statement becomes controversial in my story. My father had a tendency to give too much to others, and perhaps not realizing that being so compassionate to others meant he gave too much away of what he should actually give to his first children. Plus, his second family got too much from him. He did not realize how much was missing in his first family's home.

To compensate for my father's lack of attention to our necessities and whatever he provided to his second family and others, since my early childhood, my mother somehow made us, her children, feel happy being by ourselves and enjoy our lives in our own means. We learned how to make our own happiness because many times we tasted what we really did not want to taste: the sour feeling of betrayal.

Growing up, I learned to understand my father's personality. It hurt, but I accepted the reality. I grew up very alert to the idea that others might try to betray me. When I was in my father's pharmacy, I paid attention to people who came close to him. Being a businessman, he interacted with so many people, and also, people came to the pharmacy who were his and Daniela's friends.

I really was skeptical about Daniela's relatives' visits to the pharmacy. She had an uncle who lived in a house inside the ranch. He was a dark-skinned man, and he had a wife and so many children. This family lived in a house that was located at the corner of one of the ends of the ranch, and I think this family did not pay any rent to my father. I did not know if my father had any business with this man.

It seemed that Daniela had promised her uncle a free place to live, and living at one of the corners of the ranch, he would guard and secure the ranch as well. That's why I was always skeptical of people I felt were taking advantage of my father, like this strange man. Consequently, I learned how to recognize signs of trust or mistrust. I began to trust my intuition even if my father told me that a particular person I did not know was his friend, was working for him, or was doing business with him. I wish he had lived longer so I could have had more opportunities to tell him about my feelings concerning some of his ways, which really affected his first children and my mother.

I can't deny that my father showed concern for me and my brothers when we really had problems. For example, one day when I was thirteen years old, walking to school, I felt sad and confused. The previous week, I had got a low grade in geometry, which had never happened before. My new geometry teacher had graded my first seventh-grade test, and when I saw the low grade of 5—equivalent to a score of 50 in US schools—I silently panicked. I did not tell anyone about it. I walked back to the pharmacy, and I cried. I had always been a very good student—actually, an excellent student. I felt a kind of fear in me, and I did not understand what was happening. I learned later that my teenage hormones were acting against me.

So I went to the pharmacy, and my father was not there. He was at his ranch. I did not tell my brother Eric what I was really feeling. I just said that I needed to go home, as I had a headache. I stayed at Ipanema Pharmacy till 4:00 p.m., waiting for Eric so we could walk to the bus station. Then we went home for the day.

The next day, I woke up crying excessively, and I felt puzzled by my behavior. Then before Eric left for the pharmacy that morning, I heard my mother asking Eric to tell my father that I was not feeling well and that she was preoccupied with me. She had asked me what I was feeling. I remember telling her that I did not know. I just felt very sad. I didn't mention the grade to her. She would not understand how much that low grade affected my self-esteem.

Later in the afternoon, my father came to our house. As he entered my bedroom and saw me crying, he immediately asked me to explain to him what was happening. I told him about the geometry test and the low grade. I believe I told him that I felt humiliated, as I had never got a low grade before, and that I had missed school the previous day. I knew I was not in a condition to go to school that day either. My classes were from 1:00 p.m. to 5:00 p.m. Deep inside, I felt tired and confused. I was an A student, and I could not understand why I failed that geometry test. It was amazing how much a low grade could tear me apart.

My father sat in a chair by my bed, just listening to me. He knew that I did not have a boyfriend and that I was very young. I remember telling him that the teacher probably gave me the wrong grade. I felt as if the geometry teacher was having a psychological war with some students. I told him I did not trust that new teacher. Then he said he would go to my school and talk to the principal. It was a private Christian middle school called Ginasio São Francisco, which translates as "Saint Francisco Middle School." A husband and his wife owned it.

The next morning, my father told me that he and the principal, Senhora Ana Lucia, decided that I should stay home for about a week, as I needed some rest. Senhora Ana Lucia understood perfectly what I was feeling. My father decided that perhaps I needed to talk to a psychologist about my inner feelings to make sure I would be fine.

The next morning, my father told me that he managed to make an appointment with a psychologist for that afternoon with a nice lady he knew personally. Later that morning, I had a strange dream. In my dream, I saw two pumpkins on my bed, looking at me and smiling. As I woke up, I was really scared of the dream. The strange thing was at that time, I did not know about Halloween because it was not a Brazilian celebration. Years passed, and I became aware of spooky Halloween celebrations when I came to live in the United States. I don't know if that weird dream was a premonition, but whatever it was, it was a scary and strange dream.

I got ready for my appointment, and my father came back in the afternoon to take me to the psychologist, Sra. Alice Catapano. While I was in her medical office, she asked me why I was crying. I did not respond, so she told me to write down what I was feeling, but not in that moment; instead, I would do it at home because she knew I needed time to reflect and write down what I was really feeling.

In the next appointment, I brought to the psychologist three notebook pages detailing childhood recollections but with nothing about the geometry test grade. I surprised myself and my father as well. My notes were about the feelings of betrayal I had felt since my early childhood. The notes really translated my sadness and frustrations and how I had not accepted the reality of my mother and father's separation.

I mentioned in my notes that my father had built a ranch house for his other family and he had never thought about doing the same for my mother, my brothers, and me. Adding to the notes, I wrote about the circumstances of my father discovering that he and my mother had nothing in common. Consequently, at home, we had to "eat the bread that the devil prepared," an old Brazilian expression for when somebody, or circumstances created by another person we know or don't know, steals from us or betrays us and we feel as if we have no way out or our hands are tied behind our back.

I went to the psychologist over the period of a month; the last time I saw her, she told me I needed to help myself; I needed to cut the umbilical cord that was somehow, metaphorically speaking, attached to my mother's body. She told me that I needed to start living my life because I was a teenager and I had a lifetime ahead of me. I realized that I had to stop, or at least I had to control the sense that I was living out my mother's past suffering, frustration, and anger. When a woman is pregnant and goes through difficult times, her emotions somehow are sensed by her unborn child. It could be something spiritual as well: the unexplainable. However, real scientific experiments reveal that traumatic experiences of expectant mothers will be later reflected in their children's lives. Somehow, anger from the past and also from the present was tormenting me, and this would not bring anything good. It would not change anything for the best.

I think that perhaps before my father passed away, he was still trying to find himself. Close to the end of his life, he decided to have a hidden relationship with someone who was about twenty years younger than he was. So conceiving a child was his way of fulfilling himself again. What was sad was that he left a child without a father. His passing was unexpected—very unexpected.

CHAPTER 9

The Survival

When my father passed away, we, the Oliveira Florencios and his other children, the Santana Florencios and their mother, Daniela, who had been living with him for the past sixteen years, did not know that my father was having heart problems. At least my mother, my brothers, and me had no clue. Perhaps if my father sensed or knew something was not right with him, he never told us. I remember my father complaining about his liver and that he medicated himself with pink pills called Litrison. His fatal downturn was so quick and his heart failed so unexpectedly that another possibility was he was not aware of how serious his condition was. My father's passing was so painful for us because it was unexpected.

When my father went to a hospital after complaining about chest pain for two days, my two brothers André Filho and Eric were in Salvador, the capital of Bahia, preparing for a very difficult vestibular test. My father never thought about asking a lawyer to prepare a will. He was just forty-six years old. For us, he was too young to die of a heart attack, and I recall he told me more than once that he would live a long life because he never smoked, he never drank alcohol, and he usually went to bed by 10:00 p.m.

However, the unexpected happened, and what Ernesto told us after talking to the doctor in the small hospital in Santana was our father had had a myocardial infarction. This news was like a bombshell. It killed him in a week. On Christmas Day of 1970, he was alive and apparently well, and then on January 2, 1971, before noon, he was gone. We, his children, were so puzzled. How did this happen? It was so fast.

After he was buried, we did not talk about inheritances. Time passed, and my oldest brother, Ernesto, realized he had to deal with the pharmacy and also my father's two families' necessities—at least for the time being. Plus, he and Amanda were planning to marry the next year. Soon, we had a surprise; at least for me it was a surprise. As mentioned before, an old man started to come to the pharmacy every week after my father's passing and told Ernesto that my father had a son with his daughter and that he was my father's employee. Then Ernesto realized there really was a third woman in my father's life. So the complete picture was my father died and left behind three families.

I began to realize how much Amanda, my future sister-in-law, had to cope with her fiancé's unexpected, problematic family situation. I realized that Amanda provided Ernesto with strength to cope with so much. So many unexpected responsibilities would be coming to him as they were planning a wedding. They actually did get married a year later. However, Ernesto had to think about how he would approach Daniela about the situation and cope with three families while he was married to Amanda; eventually, they would have their own children. He had graduated as an agricultural engineer, and now, he had to apply for a new job. This would take time, so Amanda encouraged him to look for a job with the Agricultural Department of the state of Bahia. Eventually, he would have to close the pharmacy.

Amanda was an intuitive young woman. She told Ernesto that he had to be truthful with Daniela as well as with my father's supposed third father-in-law. He could not afford to sustain three families, and plus, he was on the way to start his own family. He would take care of my mother, and he knew that I had to graduate. The plan was that I would pursue a double major in Portuguese and English.

I actually did graduate with a degree in Portuguese and French in another city. For some time, my mother and I lived with Ernesto and

Amanda. Soon, Ernesto and Amanda left to live in her hometown. I stayed almost alone, as I needed to complete my degree. When I did complete it, I went to join my mother, Eric, and André in Salvador, where we lived together for a few years.

Right after my father passed away, we, the Oliveira Florencios, became sort of like gypsies, as we moved so many times and we were never together. Ernesto and Amanda decided to go start a new life in Petrolina. He had to give up his agricultural engineer job, but in Petrolina, they could build a mansion, not just a house, as Amanda's father owned a construction company. This way, they could save lots of money; in reality, this fulfilled her wishes.

When Ernesto and Amanda left Santana, Ernesto knew that Daniela would not have big problems raising her children. She was a smart woman; she had resources. She was very intuitive as well. When my father was alive, she took advantage of the situation. It seems that while my father was alive, Daniela was in control of the situation. Daniela actually had two farms and animals she raised: cows, pigs, and chickens. Plus, over the years, my father had made great investments in the huge Rancho Aurora. My father had planted so many fruit trees on Rancho Aurora that Daniela and David, her oldest son, would sell lots of mangoes and many other fruits. I came to know that the small ranch my grandmother Marilia lived on even before my father died belonged to Daniela—more surprises, at least for me.

Rancho Aurora, where Daniela had lived with my father for the past sixteen years, was huge. The area measured at least sixty thousand square meters; part was legally my father's, and part was legally hers. There were two farms, or two ranches, together. I want to emphasize that three or four years before my father passed away, he bought another farm to raise cattle, and there, eventually, he met his third woman, Iracema. Nobody ever told me her last name, and to this day, I don't know her family's name. I was told that she got married and later her husband died.

Rancho Aurora actually still exists, and the name continues to be the same. *Aurora* is a Portuguese name that translates to "Sunrise." In reality, it means "dawn" or the "first lights of the day," when we see the first light of the sun in the sky, before the actual sunrise in the east. In Portuguese, we can also understand this as *Amanhecer*.

Ernesto knew that Daniela had lots of resources; plus, in the past, she had sold some land, as she had divided a small part of the ranch into lots when I was eight or nine years old—perhaps from 1962 to 1964, or beyond that time as well. My father had helped her sell the lots. So, with my father's death, she could perhaps sell more lots of her part of Rancho Aurora, and she did.

This recollection is very painful for me. I remember that my father paid a small advertising company to help with the sales, and I also remember hearing on the radio the offering of the lots. As a child, I felt so, so betrayed. It was someone taking from me and my family. And while lying in my bed at night, I did cry, and I would tell myself, *How can my father be so, so blind? This is injustice. He has been so compassionate for others.* My thoughts were in vain.

Daniela was an ambitious woman. Before my father died, perhaps she sensed, or somebody told her, that he was having an affair away from Santana on another farm he had bought sometime in 1967 or 1968. I believe after that Daniela pressed my father to buy another small ranch, which my father used to take care of his mother, my grandmother, Marilia. Aunt Janete, my mother's sister, had come from her hometown to take care of my grandmother.

Ernesto realized the one-year-old boy, my father's last son, would also be in the picture. Today, I think about how this little boy called Alexandre Florencio survived. God took care of him. He is doing well; he is a pastor at a Christian church in Brazil and happily married with a beautiful daughter in college aspiring to be a lawyer.

After our father died, we all felt as if we were thrown into an ocean full of sharks, and we had to swim. We knew that we could not sink; we really had to swim, so day by day, we all learned how to survive. The Lord has his mysterious ways to show to his children on earth that life is not just a sea of roses. That's how we learn we are humans and we have a mind with which to think. We have intuition; sometimes, we preview what is coming down our path, and finally, we know when we have to make serious and important decisions.

A week after my father died, Eric and André Filho went to Salvador for their tests. Soon after, they got the results for the scary vestibular. Eric passed the tests. André Filho did not. Eric had applied to study architecture. André had applied for system analyses engineering, which was a very challenging, in-demand area at the time and a new trend in Brazil. In both areas, the bar for a student to pass the tests was very high, and Eric and André knew it would be a challenge.

When Eric received the good news, I believe he cried because our father had just passed away and he needed so much to pass the tests. I knew that God was by the boys' side; however, just one of them, Eric, was granted the good news. Since Eric's childhood, I remember always seeing him with crayons, rulers, colored pencils, and paper; whenever he could, he kept his supplies with him, as he loved to design, draw, and color. He was good at graphic design. There were no computers at the time. He drew by hand. He used to draw with passion, and I am sure he was born gifted in this particular area. Eric studied at Bahia Federal University to become an architect, and he knew it would take him at least five years to complete the program. He was aware he had to work as well. And he did.

André soon found a job as an administrative assistant for a construction company. Then a few years later, he married Camilla, a beautiful young lady from South Bahia. Then he and Camilla planned to live in London. André had researched a system analyses one-year intensive program at Oxford University in England. Camilla's father at the time was a mayor in one of the small towns in South Bahia and financially helped his daughter and son-in-law, yet André paid for his classes, as he had saved for this purpose before traveling to England.

I continued my studies in high school. After graduation, I began studies in the only faculty in Santana that offered a two-and-a-half-year program for aspiring middle school teachers. I completed one year of studies, and then Ernesto talked to me and to my mother about coming to live with him and Amanda in the city where he would be working as an agricultural engineer. I had to transfer to the Portuguese-French middle school teaching program. There was no Portuguese-English program, although that was my intention. I got the degree, yet before my graduation Ernesto and Amanda decided to live in Petrolina, the city located by the San Francisco River, which divides the cities of Juazeiro, in the state of Bahia, and Petrolina, which belongs to the state of Pernambuco.

As previously mentioned, Daniela managed to raise her children. David finished high school, got a job, and then later he got married, bought a truck, and continued to work selling sodas and beers to small restaurants surrounding the ranch. Fernando moved to Salvador, as it was, and is, a big city with job opportunities, and he managed to take two-year classes at a technical college. Later he opened his own business offering residential owners and businesses air-conditioner maintenance. He and his girl friend rented an apartment and decided to live together. Soon they had a son.

Samantha and Lívia got married very young. They had simple country lives. Samantha managed to go to college to become a teacher. As mentioned before, she also managed to get a PhD in Pedagogy. Daniela gave her daughters, Samantha and Lívia, two lots, and then both of them, with their husbands, managed to build their houses inside of Rancho Aurora and be neighbors. They raised their children without the costs of a big city like Salvador, where Fernando lives. Eliana later finished college and graduated.

They live on the ranch without the preoccupations of a big city. The cost of living was and still is less expensive for them. My father and Daniela planted mangoes, oranges, tangerines, jaca trees, and many other fruit trees that even today exist on Rancho Aurora. A jaca is a huge tropical fruit, and I believe it's just found in Brazil. Each tree my father planted provided enormous shade to the front of the ranch house and throughout the ranch. He and Daniela used to plant lots of vegetables as well. My father could afford to pay many country people to work on the farm.

The fruit trees have been there for at least sixty years. And I believe Daniela must have planted other things and flowers also. Some of the fruits were used to feed the animals. In the countryside, life is easy. I remember my father constantly saying that Santana and Rancho Aurora were the best places to live in the world. It was for him, not for me or my brothers and my mother.

* * *

January 1971 and afterward, Ernesto had serious talks with Daniela. He told Daniela that he could not have a lawyer deal with the will. And the idea was to eventually divide the ranch into lots—actually, my father's half the huge land because it would be very expensive. Ernesto eventually would leave to take care of his own life. He was on the way to marrying Amanda. He reminded Daniela that she had to be strong to continue her life without my father. He told her that she was blessed to have possessions with which to take care of her children. At the time, my mother was the one who needed her sons, and I needed Ernesto's support to continue my studies and eventually graduate and get a job, perhaps as a teacher.

For Daniela, Rancho Aurora was a gold mine. It's amazing how much she managed to take from my father to build a nest for her and her children. I guess I learned from her as well. I became a very intuitive person. Today, my intuition is strong. I sense people's intentions as being good or bad. Daniela's betrayal began much before I was conceived and born; perhaps because of this situation, I became intuitive.

A year and a half after my father's passing, Ernesto finally closed the pharmacy when he and Amanda got married. Their wedding happened on the beautiful morning of December 31, 1971. All the family was present, including Daniela's children, except Eliana, as she was very young at the time. The wedding was a day of happiness for all of us: the Oliveira Florencios, Amanda's family, and the Santana Florencios. I believe that we fulfilled our father's wishes that we, the Oliveira Florencios and Santana Florencios, shouldn't be enemies. We actually continued our lives the way he left us. He wanted us to know that his children with Daniela were not guilty of the situation he and Daniela created. We did not forget the sour taste in our lives. I guess we forgave it.

Anyway, a new chapter began for Ernesto and Amanda. Their wedding was a celebration on a sunny morning in the huge, white Petrolina Cathedral on the banks of the San Francisco River. Looking to the other side of the river, we could see the other city, Juazeiro. Juazeiro is named after a tree. The name *Petrolina* comes from *petra*, a Latin word that means "rock," or actually *pedra* in Portuguese. So Petrolina is the "City of Rock," not rock and roll but a real rock. This is just a small geography lesson about Brazil, the largest country in South America.

This small part of this chapter is perhaps the translation of the happiness felt at Ernesto and Amanda's wedding a year after my father's passing. However, this is a psychological memoir of a young girl telling her story and her father's story as well. I am Katia, the little girl, and André was my father. I want to say that I never said I hated my father. In my own way, I loved him. My wish is that while he was alive, he could have done for his first children what he did for his others.

CHAPTER 10

The Will

Sixteen years later, finally, Eric and David got together and decided to plan for the will. The huge ranch was in danger because poor people were invading it, building makeshift little cabanas on it because no wall protected the ranch; there were just fences made of twisted wire and old wood around the entire ranch. By 1988, after my youngest son, Alan, was born, I received a call from André, my youngest brother, saying that Eric was planning to finally prepare our father's will, as his construction business was doing very well and he could afford to go ahead with his plans. He decided to put his own money toward paying for a lawyer and other professionals to divide our father's part of the ranch into lots, so legally, my mother would have 50 percent of the sales of the lots, and the other 50 percent would be subdivided by his children. As far as I can recall, André told me on the phone that Daniela was preoccupied with the situation she saw unfolding behind the ranch. Almost every day, she walked around the huge land, where the two ranches had been one since 1955 or 1956.

Eric knew that taking care of my father's will would be advantageous for us, the Oliveira Florencios, as opposed to the Santana Florencios, because my mother never divorced my father. We all knew that my father had pressed my mother to get a divorce in 1963 and 1964. At the time, at least Ernesto, being the oldest child in our house, knew that my father had some fishy plans, and probably was in favor of Daniela; today, I think he probably did not know about Daniela's evil intentions at the time. Or he never did.

Some people are just evil. Some women are very manipulative, and they always find a way to throw poison at a relationship, especially when they live in the couple's house and spy everything. That was what Daniela did to my mother. She figured out that my mother was naïve; she spied on my mother's ways and discovered my mother's weaknesses, such as reading slowly and getting confused by simple math facts—what I came to understand much later when working with slow-level-development students. So day by day, Daniela determined that to get André Florencio, my father, she just had to jump in at the right moment. So Daniela acted as a smooth operator, like the song we all know.

Per my mother's recollections when she remembered things (not anymore, as she is showing signs of Alzheimer's), the story was that Daniela came to live in our house after August 1951. Then she spied on our family. She secretly planned to run away with my father, André. I think she felt a certain jealousy because her mother, Soraya, never married the man who was Daniela's father. She was conceived out of wedlock. Perhaps she wanted some kind of revenge against the world around her and the Oliveira Florencios became her victims.

I hadn't been conceived yet in 1951, but perhaps the angels were planning to have me coming soon and, one day, they would lead me to write this memoir to alert women out there of poisonous and quietly dragging snakes. So a woman who decides to live with a married man with children signifies trouble—and days and years of fight and torment. When I was very young, I never asked my father questions. By twelve or thirteen years old, I never dared to confront him, but after that, I remember I started to ask many *why* questions. I used to think that everything belonged to him and that Daniela had robbed us of him and was just using him.

* * *

By the end of 1988, Eric and David managed to pay a lawyer to prepare a sort of probate, or actually the will, to match Eric's resolution to legally divide the half of Rancho Aurora that legally belonged to my father, and another professional came to design and divide the lots, the topography. The new document was called, in Portuguese, Loteamento Irmãos Florencio, which in English translates to "Florencio *Brothers* Property Lots." I cannot exactly translate the words into English because, in this case, the lots included both the sons and the daughters of André Florencio, meaning all his children.

The document was prepared. It took time and money to work on the land to physically divide the lots, create and pave the new streets, and add the needed lights to illuminate the area before David started selling the lots. Eric advanced the money needed for the project. I believe it took almost ten years for David to sell a great part of the property.

After I moved to the United States, sometime in 1986, my brother Eric sent me a document to sign so he could sell our house, the one our father had bought for us. This was the house he bought for us in a state of emergency when the bedroom wall of an old house we lived in fell down. After the sale of our house in Santana, Eric bought a small house for my mother in a city called Maceió, where he; his wife, Susana; and his three children, Jonas, Carlos, and Dilon, live.

Eric and Susana live in two houses. From Monday to Friday, they are in a town house because Susana works in her medical office very close to the town house and Eric works in civil construction, and on weekends, they spend their time in their nice beach house, which is located in a quiet and deserted area very close to the ocean. There are coconut trees all over this beach. These trees grow like pine trees do in Georgia. It seems that the wind blows the seeds all over the place and they naturally grow.

When I left Brazil in February 1985, my mother went to live with Ernesto and Amanda and then with André and Camilla, and then she lived by herself for perhaps just a year. By June 1988, she was already living in Maceió in a very small house. She did not complain—at least she did not complain to me. Probably she did not complain to anybody. It was her own house. I was the one who felt uncomfortable with the size and look of the house.

I came to the United States in February 1985, now Katia Florencio Parker, with my first son, Benjamin, and my husband, Benjamin Parker III. When I traveled to Brazil for the first time after Alan, my second son, was born, I visited my three brothers, my sisters-in-law, and my nephews and nieces. When I returned to Brazil with my two sons (Alan was just ten months old, and Benjamin was almost three years old), I walked into my mother's house, and for some reason, I felt sad. The house was very small and poor looking. I mentioned to Eric that I was saddened by the house he bought. What Eric told me was that when he tried to sell our house in Santana, he realized it was impossible to get a good price for it, as it had not been maintained in years. He managed to get it painted, but it needed fixing. However, it was not worth the cost.

We talked, and I believe I told him that I hoped that with the selling of the lots, he would be able to build our mother a nice house. He was an architect, and his business was civil construction. I could not promise anything. I just prayed to God for a miracle. I thought that perhaps Eric could sell the small house and build a better one. We really needed a miracle.

When the Brazilian government found a way for two years, 1998 and 1999, to have the Brazilian money called real changed and valued as the US dollar, the miracle came. People were buying and selling properties and building houses and traveling. Finally, David found an opportunity to sell many lots, with one US dollar equal to one real. I cannot clearly explain how this happened. It became more expensive for foreigners to obtain the real in money exchanges before traveling to Brazil when they needed it in transactions.

Again, I have to say that God works in mysterious ways. During 1998 and 1999, many people from Brazil traveled extensively to the United States, probably mostly to Miami and New York to shop. During this time, while the Brazilian economy was strong, David managed to sell many lots, and Eric was constantly traveling to Santana to stay informed about the sales and get some money, as he really was planning to build a house for my mother. Eventually, Eric got his money back by selling the lots, as David took advantage of the opportunity created by the good economic state of the country. Later, sometime in October

1999, I made a surprise trip to Brazil. The company I was working for told me that I could take some time off before Christmas, and actually, I did. I surprised my family. I told them I was on the way to Brazil just a few days before leaving the United States.

Eric and David constantly saw each other, and I think a brotherhood and friendship really solidified between them then. I know that while we were growing up, my father always told us not to point at each other and say that one or the other was guilty of anything. Always, I felt my father's preoccupation that one day we, his children from both families, could end up being enemies. It never happened because I guess my father let us know that we all were his children. He was the provider in our house despite the years we moved from house to house without having our own place while he lived in his comfortable ranch house with the Santana Florencios.

So the Oliveira Florencios and Santana Florencios lived in harmony. I can't deny that many times I choked as if I was eating something sour when I was young. I used to feel betrayed by my father and Daniela. The reality is that, we, the Oliveira Florencios and Santana Florencios, had and still have good relationships with each other. We are my father's children even if he did not live with us and our mother in our home; instead, the other ones were the blessed ones.

We could, however, see him every day in the pharmacy. I believe my father conceived the idea that the pharmacy was *his* house, not Daniela's or my mother's house. There, he brought all his children together. Perhaps metaphorically speaking, it was a church where the priest or pastor reunites everyone despite their differences, as following Christian teachings. The pharmacy was one of my father's places of happiness. The other one was Rancho Aurora.

We worked with him and helped him in the pharmacy, as it was the place where he felt comfortable resolving issues with his children. At one time, perhaps four or five years before he died, when Ernesto left for Juazeiro to be a student at the agricultural college by the San Francisco River, my father decided to open another pharmacy in Santana not so far from Ipanema. He passed on the responsibilities of taking care of the small pharmacy to Eric, who was taking night classes at a local high school at the time. He named the pharmacy

Farmácia Brilho do Sol. It was located on a street corner not so far from Igreja Nosso Senhor dos Passos, which in English can be translated as "Church of Our Lord of the Small Steps."

I think that Eric was happy about this decision, as he had decided to attend night classes so he could work in the new small pharmacy during the day and go to class at night. Somehow, three years before my father passed away, in 1967 or 1968, he closed Ipanema Pharmacy, the big one that our father had had since 1954, and he came to work with Eric in the small Farmácia Brilho do Sol.

By August 1985, after becoming a mother for the first time, deep inside, I decided to forgive my father's actions. Perhaps I had forgiven him when he died many years before, when I was just sixteen years old. At home, my family had sometimes struggled to have basic necessities, as my father was the provider for so many people. When I was five and my father was driving me to the ranch house for the first time, he said, "You will like it. It's our new house." Even as a child, I knew that what he was saying was not true. Everything that was happening was just false. That house was not my house.

I remember Daniela saying to me, "I am glad you are here, and I want you to know that you are like my daughter." I knew as a five-year-old that the place was not mine. It was internally torturous. I had to pretend and not cry; as a child, I did not want to show jealousy or weakness. I suppose I was confused by reality.

My first real recollections of my life come from when I was five. I recall seeing my mother crying every afternoon after we all ate lunch and after she cleaned the kitchen. I recall seeing my mother sitting in a chair in our first old house, looking at her little girl playing with dolls and miniature furniture, with little tables, chairs, and the tablecloth and small plastic flowers to enhance the doll's house. I was witness to my mother's tears. Yet my father perhaps never really understood how much he had hurt his first children, and the one who felt most hurt probably was me. I guess that's because I had brothers, and as boys, they grew up listening to people say that boys should not cry or show weakness and that boys should act as if everything is fine.

We children knew that the house and the part of the ranch that belonged to Daniela were just symbols of betrayal, and her words were of sarcasm and lies. The situation was like trick-or-treat. If you just gave a child some candy, he or she would be fine. The next day, the candy would be gone, but the raw reality would still be there.

While in my mother's womb, my spirit as a developing child heard my mother's cries and really felt her emotions. Perhaps much before the conception, I was present. Perhaps an angel wanted to be born upon hearing the claims of a suffering woman. A certain spirit was levitating without anybody seeing it. Before I came from my mother's womb, I was already present in spirit. The spirit of an angel alerted the future child to be strong and protect the mother. It alerted the child about the truth—the betrayal that had already happened.

Perhaps when my father found out that my mother was expecting a child, seven or eight months before I was born, he tried to deny my existence. If he did, he must have had regrets—lots of regrets. Who knows? Perhaps while in the hospital, sensing that his spirit could no longer support his body in the last days or last moments of his existence, he had regrets. I recall seeing him cry when Amanda and I came to visit him the day before he passed away. Just God knows.

I've come to believe that there was an angel hovering over my home. The reality was that my mother wanted to have a little girl, as she told me when I could understand human language. She wanted God to bring her a small companion, a daughter. Perhaps her spirit wanted revenge. Perhaps she thought that my father did not love her or never did, and so a child, a little girl, would be part of him. This would be something that Daniela never could take away from her. Probably these thoughts crossed her mind before I even was conceived. Actually, she told me about her prayers to God to bring her a little girl. I guess God and the angels heard her and I was born as a result.

* * *

Eric realized that the moment was coming for him to build my mother's dream house with the sale of the lots coming from my father's inheritance. So even before the lots were ready to be sold, Eric was seriously making plans to build the house. I am sure Eric thought that now he would have what we had for so long waited for. We, all my mother's children, were waiting for an opportunity to give our mother a nice new place to live. Building her new house would make up for the years of betrayal. It would not really erase the sorrows that Daniela and my father had provoked.

It was a family *conquista* (a Portuguese word used when someone conquers something). It was 1999, and then the construction of the house was delayed into the year 2000. It took so long; however, Eric finally saw an opportunity to build my mother's house. Before, in my mother's small house, she was unable to receive her children's or grandchildren's visits. We would go there briefly, and then we went to Eric's town house and sometimes the beach house. I suppose that perhaps Eric mentioned to David that I was sad when I came to visit my mother for the first time after my sons were born. I saw our mother living in a poor-looking house, so we, her children, felt that now was the time to make up for the long years of waiting.

I am sure that Eric told David about his plans. He was and still is an architect, and he was the one who invested in the ranch to be divided into lots. So the construction of our mother's house was the first priority. Then we, the heirs, had to trust Eric and David to deal with the sale and division of the lots. David was born on Rancho Aurora, and he knew lots of people who lived in the area. I believe this helped to sell the lots, along with the good times caused by the Brazilian government making changes in the Brazilian currency, with the real reaching the same value as the US dollar.

Many times, André emailed me, as David was very busy with the negotiations. I believe Eric, David, and André had projected if all lots were sold, all parties—each of us—would have a great amount of money, according to the will. Eric was really committed to building a nice house for my mother. From 1998 to 1999, Eric managed to build Susana's medical office, taking advantage of the good times when the real was strong. Then later, from 1999 to 2000, Eric managed to build our mother's house. Finally, the dream came true. It was for a good cause. Our mother finally had a nice place to live.

CHAPTER 11

The Road to Heaven

When I visited my family in May and June 2011, while I spent a few days in Petrolina with Ernesto, Amanda, and their two daughters, Lenize and Tatiana, they invited me to come back for their wedding anniversary in December. They planned to invite all the family: the Rodrigueses, who were Amanda's family; the Oliveira Florencios; the Santana Florencios; and many of Amanda's and Ernesto's friends. I knew that I could not go back again in 2011.

When I got home to the United States, I talked to my children, Alan and Benjamin, about the possibility of going to Brazil to visit our family, and then for the last week, they could stay in Petrolina with Uncle Ernesto and Aunt Amanda for their wedding anniversary. Michael, Ernesto and Amanda's oldest child, lived in the north of the country. He was married and had two daughters. Michael; his wife, Carolina; and their children were planning to come to the wedding anniversary as well.

When I returned to Brazil for the first time in 1988 with my two sons, Alan was just ten months old, and Benjamin was almost three. Then we returned to Brazil quite a few times together while they were growing up. However, neither of them had traveled to Brazil alone before. Alan speaks Spanish and Portuguese quite fluently. Benjamin still struggles with Portuguese. Alan studied Spanish during his four years in high school, which greatly helped him to learn and speak Portuguese, and he was excited to practice his Portuguese in Brazil without having me, his mother, by his side. Benjamin had taken two years of German, so he missed Spanish, which would have given him a good foundation to learn Portuguese, as these languages are very similar in structure and pronunciation. We didn't speak much Portuguese when they were growing up.

Alan said that he liked the idea, as he had worked constantly for the past year without any breaks since leaving Georgia State University and perhaps he could plan the trip to Brazil in advance. He was very excited, as it would be his first trip to Brazil by himself. Then after much planning and shopping, by the second week of December 2011, I took Alan to the airport in Atlanta, and he flew on American Airlines. He planned to fly from Atlanta to Miami and then to Salvador. His uncle André would be the first person to pick him up at the airport in Salvador, as Alan would be arriving via a straight flight from Miami. On his return trip, he would leave Salvador, and then he would go to São Paulo, Miami, and finally Atlanta.

When Alan got to Salvador, his uncle André was there waiting for him. When they arrived at André and Camilla's apartment, Alan called me, and briefly, we talked. He was tired yet excited to be in Salvador. It was raining. We planned to talk using Skype while he stayed in Brazil.

Soon after lunch, André took Alan to Pelourinho to see Old Bahia. This downtown area is where the Portuguese built the first houses in the city. It's the oldest area in the capital city. This area has many Catholic churches, residential houses, and old buildings still being used for businesses. There is also an area called Cidade Alta uptown, and the Cidade Baixa area is downtown. To go to the downtown area, people walk past the governor's palace to take the Elevador Lacerda, which is a huge elevator.

People may also take the Plano Inclinado, which is like a small sky lift. The sky lift in Salvador was and still is an option to move from uptown to downtown. It's not as big as a sky lift in Atlanta that goes up to Stone Mountain or in Switzerland that goes up to the Alps. It's somehow small. A Swiss company engineered it many years ago. In the past, there were also *bondes* that resembled small trains that ran on tracks. They were similar to the transportation now available in Atlanta that many tourists and residents use, taking advantage of it to avoid driving in traffic. It's interesting to see the sky lifts, actually made up of two old machines, moving. Using the balance of the two small parts that resemble buses or trains, the parts create a balance as they move. When one goes up, the other goes down. It's an old sky lift design.

As soon as people get off the Plano Inclinado, walking across a block and an old garden, they see the old Mercado; actually, it's called the Mercado Modelo. There, tourists buy souvenirs, and at the old restaurant upstairs at the Mercado, tourists taste foods typical of the land: Caruru, Vatapá, Acarajé, Abará, and other Afro-Brazilian foods like Ensopado de Peixe com Leite de Côco ("fish with coconut milk"), which are typical Comidas Baianas ("foods of Bahia"). Coconut milk is added to many Comidas Baianas. Also, a vegetable oil called Azeite de Dendê—a reddish, natural-color oil typical of Bahia—is added to food, mostly seafood. It has a unique flavor.

It is said that close to this old Mercado, or old market, slaves were sold when they came in big ships that anchored in Porto de Salvador very close by. This area is at least 450 years old. I went there with Alan when he was thirteen years old and again when he was around twenty years old when we visited Brazil without Benjamin. So Alan has more recollections of Brazil than Ben. Alan spent a few days in Salvador sightseeing. He bought some souvenirs before his flight back to the United States.

In 2012, Ben and I traveled to Brazil for a family wedding. We spent just one week there, so Ben does not have many memories of Brazil. I preserve the memories with pictures we took on our vacations while he was younger. Before the 2012 trip, he had been there when he was thirteen years old. After a few days in Salvador, Alan took a bus to Juazeiro, and then the bus crossed the San Francisco River and reached Petrolina, where Ernesto and Amanda were preparing for the big party to celebrate their fortieth wedding anniversary.

It was an unforgettable experience for Alan. During the party, Michael's father-in-law sent a message to Ernesto and Amanda wishing them happiness. To Alan's surprise, Michael asked him to read a kind of speech. Alan told me that the message was, of course, in Portuguese; Michael wanted people to see Alan speaking in Portuguese. Months later, while in Brazil, Michael showed me a small video he made, and I could see my son Alan reading the message in Portuguese in front of so many people, family and friends. I could see that David and Fernando and both their wives, Danuze and Pauliana, were there; also, I saw Eliana and Suely, Eliana's youngest daughter. Samantha; her husband, Francisco; and their daughter Sheila were there as well. So most of the Santana Florencios were at the party. I could see many of the Rodrigues family members, as they live in the city as well.

When Alan came back to the United States, he told me about the party, and months later, I was happy to see the video Michael arranged to be put together of the family celebrating Ernesto and Amanda's happiness in enjoying their wedding anniversary joined by their children, family, and friends. It was the last day of the year, December 31, 2011. I realized it was a great party. Everybody enjoyed the celebration very much. Alan also told me about his experience flying alone to Brazil and the excitement he experienced at the airport in Sao Paulo on his way back. He almost missed his international flight from Sao Paulo to Miami buying souvenirs for us.

* * *

Almost a month had passed since Alan came back from Brazil, and if I recall correctly, on the third Saturday morning, while I was still in bed resting by ten in the morning (11:00 a.m. in Brazil), the phone rang. I got the phone and said, "Hello?"

A voice answered, in Portuguese, "Alô!" which means, "Hello!"

I recognized that it was my brother André, so I quickly said to him, "Oi André, tudo bom? Uma vez mais, muito obrigado pela estadia de Alan na sua casa." This translates as "Hi, André. Is everything okay? Once more, thank you very much for having Alan at your home."

André sounded sad and tense. He said, "Katia, what I have to tell you is not good. A few hours ago, David had an accident, and he did not survive."

I heard André's words; however, I was in disbelief. So, I asked, "What happened?" Then he told me that David; his wife, Danuze; and Eric had driven to Monte Feliz to spend a few days there and show Danuze the city where our father, André Florencio; our mother, Diana; and David's mother, Daniela, were born. Monte Feliz is the city that we, the first four children of André Florencio, the Oliveira Florencios, were born in as well.

He continued. "There, they stayed in a small country hotel, and then they rented three horses so they could ride in the fields and in the city, and they were planning to go as far as they could up to Monte Feliz, actually up on the mountain." Monte Feliz is named after the mountain of the same name. Then he said, "I don't know too many of the details; however, Eric just called me crying, saying that the horses David and Danuze were riding on began to run too fast, and they could not control them. It seems that while the horses were running, David and Danuze were thrown off because of the horses' speed. Both did not survive. Camilla is preparing our suitcases. We have to travel to Santana as soon as possible. An ambulance already got to the field in Monte Feliz where they were. At this moment, I suppose one or two ambulances are bringing the corpses to Santana." Finally, he said, "I have to go. I'll talk to you later. Good-bye."

Then I said, "Good-bye."

Alan and my husband, Benjamin, were home. I talked to them briefly; then I decided to call Ernesto in Brazil. It's much easier for me to call my family in Brazil than for them to call me. From there, it's more expensive, especially if they use a cell phone. When I called Ernesto, he told me that, by coincidence, Michael was spending a few days with them and that Susana, my brother Eric's wife, had called to tell him about the accident. So Ernesto, Amanda, and Michael were getting ready to drive to Santana. The drive would take about six hours. They planned to drive instead of fly, as they had their car. Also, there were no straight flights from Petrolina to Santana or from Santana to Petrolina. Petrolina has a relatively big airport, but Santana has just a small airport for small planes, and even today, there are no flights between these two cities. They would have to take at least two flights; plus, they would have to rent a car.

That night, January 25, I did not sleep well, as I was in disbelief. I could not call Daniela, and I knew I could not call Samantha, Fernando, Lívia, or Eliana. I knew they were in shock. And I was preoccupied by thoughts about Eric. I asked myself, *How is Eric handling himself?* I knew that his wife was a doctor. However, Eric was the one who was riding a horse along with David and Danuze.

The trip was supposed to be a relaxing one—a small vacation surrounded by nature—so why did God let this happen? All night long, I kept thinking about David, and I kept thinking about Daniela, his mother, the one who took my mother almost to insanity. So many things crossed my mind. Was this a punishment for Daniela? But in this case, David was gone. Everything that happened in the past was not David's fault. If the angels wanted revenge, they would have taken Daniela, not David. David was Daniela's most precious possession. He was her first son—the son who was conceived over my mother's cross. The past was my mother's crucifixion. I know that my mother does not remember too much about the past now; however, I know that she did not wish anything bad to happen to my father and Daniela's children.

I just could not process the idea that David was gone. I kept thinking, *How fast and unexpectedly can a person just die?*

When I was a child, my mother used to tell me, "Every morning when you wake up, you must pray Our Father Who Art in Heaven and the Hail Mary." At night, she used to tell me that I should do my prayers again because evil could be around; we never knew when the evil spirit would catch us or tempt us. When I grew up, I never forgot my mother's simple words.

My grandfather, Leonardo Oliveira, an Italian descendent and a Catholic by faith, taught my mother to fear God. I think my grandfather meant that having a fear in God means to respect our Creator, the Great Spirit of Light that gives us comfort and peace. I remember my mother and my father always telling me, "If you are in need, if you feel you are in despair, silently and quietly you must reach him, our God," because both my parents' fathers and mothers taught them to reach God anytime you feel you are in need. So I grew up learning what prayers are for. Also, my father used to tell me that those who believe in God will not fall. I think these words came from my grandfather André Senior to my father.

After David and his wife's accident, I began to think seriously about life and how life can be cut short or take unexpected turns. I began recollecting my parents' teachings about God from when I was raised as a Christian. I respect other religions, but I do not follow any other religion. I am a Catholic, so I am a Christian. I know that each person is free to pursue his or her own devotions, as most people follow their parents' religion or creed. So being a Christian followed my parents' religion; it was their creed even if my mother was Catholic and my father grew up Presbyterian. I chose to be a Christian and a Catholic.

When I am in the city of Maceió in Brazil, l always take my elderly mother to a chapel that has weekly services on Wednesdays. It's very rewarding for me to go to this small church with my ninety-two-year-old mother. I don't know how long she will live. She did live twice as long as my father, as he died when he was forty-six years old.

Perhaps the difficult part of living is that I haven't completely grasped the silent and mysterious ways of God. I ask myself why David left so early. Was his death a punishment for his mother's choices? I don't have the answer. I always remember my mother's words: "Pray to God. Fear and respect him, and watch your steps." One thing I know is that day by day, as we get older, we acquire intuition. I believe this is one of God's great gifts. Sometimes, we perceive things before they happen. However, sometimes we can be wrong. The best thing perhaps is not to say what has crossed our minds. I see that as many people get older, they get more and more intuitive. It's true. I guess I am getting old but not too old yet. I am getting wise—very wise.

CHAPTER 12

The Inheritance

Two weeks after David's passing, I decided to call Samantha, who I knew was still in shock. I thought, *I have to be very careful about what I say.* So when I called her, I was cautious about what I said and asked about the accident. When she answered, I asked her how her mother and everyone else were coping with the loss of David. She said that her mother was still in shock; of course, she was in a state of disbelief, and she hadn't stopped crying. I could sense in Samantha's words that because David was her first son, Daniela loved him perhaps much more than her other children.

David had lived on Rancho Aurora since he was born. When my father had bought the two ranches and made one huge ranch out of them named Rancho Aurora, he legally registered the deed for the first ranch in his name, and he registered the second one, bought from the neighbor, in Daniela's name. It was his first big gift for her.

When my father bought the first ranch, he found three small and simple houses; he and Daniela lived in one of them for three or four years. Later, he let one of his employees, an old lady called Senhora Nancy, live on the ranch. Senhora Nancy used to work on the ranch, taking care of Daniela's animals. Senhora Nancy also planted and watered Daniela's plants and flowers. Ten years later, when he bought a farm far away from Santana, planning to raise cattle, he took Senhora Nancy to live in the farm's small house. He started to go to this farm once a week on Wednesdays. Senhora Nancy lived on the new farm for at least three years until my father died unexpectedly in the beginning of 1971.

Initially, Daniela and my father lived in one of the little houses and rented the two other ones. Soon after buying the second ranch, they started to plan for the construction of their dream house. I believe Fernando and Lívia were also born in the same little house as David. My father had already named the first ranch Rancho Aurora. When Daniela was pregnant with Samantha, they planned to build the new ranch house before the arrival of the new baby girl. And their plans worked. My father, Daniela and their first three children - David, Fernando and Livia moved to the new ranch house before the arrival of Samantha. Later, in March 1964 Eliana was born.

Many years after my father died, perhaps in 1979 and 1980, David built a house in a lot on the ranch given to him by his mother. By then, he and his wife, Danuze, were happy, as they were living right there, neighboring Rancho Aurora. Daniela had divided and sold some lots, perhaps when my father was alive or after he passed away, when she found herself raising her children alone. David's house was not built by Daniela's house, as Samantha's and Lívia's houses were. The girls could even walk to their mother's house at any time of day or night. I guess it was more secure for all of them; if anything happened to their mother or grandmother, they would be just a few steps from each other's homes.

One night, after living in the house for about a year, David, Danuze, and their young first son, Josué, had gone out, and when they got back at night, David was attacked by a robber. He was taken to a hospital, and soon after surgery, by the grace of God, he recuperated well. However, David and Danuze decided not to live in the house anymore. Danuze felt very scared, as she was with him and their son when the robber attacked her husband. They sold the house because it was not safe anymore, or it never had been.

The ranch was located in a poor neighborhood. The streets were not well lit. With the area growing because of many new residences, they had to move away very quickly. It was a good decision to sell their property and move away. Before selling his house, David told his mother that he would like to build a small house right by where she lived. It would be safe for Danuze and their little boy. He was planning to just expand her ranch house, building a wall to separate the two houses. Daniela asked him to build a small house for her instead of for them. He, Danuze, and their son, and also perhaps more children, could live in her house, and she would live in the new small house, as she just needed two small bedrooms: one for her and one for her sick mother. Her aunt had died a few years before.

So David, Danuze, and their little boy moved into Daniela's ranch house, where Samantha and Eliana had been born. They were happy for the change. Actually, it was much better and safer for the little boy to be close to his grandmother. Danuze planned to get a job or perhaps have another child. Eventually, the job would come. Her son would be safe right there, in the same place where his father grew up.

* * *

When I talked to Samantha on the phone, I believe two weeks after David passed away, Samantha was sad and tense, and she told me her mother was not accepting the reality that David was gone. Samantha said that she had taken two weeks off of work to take care of her mother. Lívia and Samantha were taking turns, as Lívia was a neighbor as well. They needed to comfort Daniela and assure her that they were by her side; she had to pick herself up and not give up on life because she had them and their grandchildren and they needed her as the matriarch of their family.

Samantha had told me a few years prior that she believed in spirituality; for example, if somebody died unexpectedly, it was because of God's plans. She told me that she had told her mother about her beliefs, which I suppose had changed over the years. She didn't just have beliefs about the death of the body. She believed that when people die, they can come back in spirit to visit their family or the ones they met during their journey on earth.

At the time, I was unable to answer her statement. I told her that God has mysterious ways for teaching us about life. Yet I continued, saying there are things that just happen—for example, a loved one's accident—and we wonder why the loved one didn't survive. I said that we cannot prove certain things to others concerning a spiritual being coming to visit us, as she had implied in our conversation. I said that I could not be sure about my last statement about the afterlife. I just told her that my mother and I, and her mother as well, being Catholics, believe that God has a plan for all of us. I learned that we must pray to him and believe in him.

During our phone conversation, I told Samantha that when André called me the day of the accident and told me the truth, I also was in disbelief. I said I felt as if David was still alive and he had just gone on a vacation or that whenever I visited them from then on, I would feel as if he was just out of the house and he would come back for lunch or later in the evening. I was about to end the conversation by telling Samantha that next May I planned to visit the family in Brazil and that I would stop at Rancho Aurora for a brief visit when suddenly Samantha's voice changed as if she was angry—very angry.

She told me she did not want anybody to call her asking about the leftover lots that David hadn't sold. I could not believe what I had just heard, as the family was going through such a difficult moment, especially her, her mother, Lívia, Eliana, and Fernando. I told her it was not the moment to talk about the leftover lots. As I am intuitive, I knew she was implying that I should not call again to ask about the situation with our inheritance. Her words sounded like an order. I did not have any intention of calling her again to talk about the leftover lots because I knew that André and Eric would probably wait a few months while mourning David's death. I did not say a word to Samantha even as things crossed my mind. It was not the moment. I knew that André, who lived two hours away from Rancho Aurora in the capital of Salvador, would contact Eric, Ernesto, Fernando, and all of us.

Then I was the one in disbelief. I felt embarrassed; I never thought she would talk about inheritances when David had just passed away two weeks before. On the phone, I pretended that I did not understand her motives in talking about these lots. However, I knew why she was telling me these things when we all were grieving for David, especially herself, as his sister. I just said good-bye, and I told her not to worry about that. Then I became preoccupied by what Samantha had said. Even if the family was going through an agonizing moment, after a few days, I called André, and I explained the conversation we had had to him. I told André about my suspicions, as my intuition was telling me something.

Samantha was trying to uphold documents that legally she shouldn't. Actually, she told me that she had gone to David and Danuze's house right there, a step away from where she lived, and found the documents we all had signed, giving him the right to sell the lots. She said that she brought them to her house because she did not want her mother to be involved in our family business. She also told me that she had an idea. She knew an attorney, and she was going to send an email to Eric and all the brothers and sisters explaining her plans.

We all trusted Eric; however, Samantha was showing an unusual interest in gaining Eric's trust so he would accept her plan. He managed to pay or lend some money on behalf of all of us to prepare the will and deal with the many things needed to divide the lots that would become our assets. We had signed a power of attorney giving David authority to negotiate the selling of the lots. I sensed that André had become suspicious of Samantha's intentions as well. I felt sad because she did not even wait to mourn her own brother's death. I sensed she was mad at the world or she was mad with the Oliveira Florencios. For me, it was clear she wanted control over our assets.

* * *

A month passed; then I called André to get an update on the situation. I told André that after my conversation with Samantha, I sensed that she was angry with the world following David's death or that perhaps she was angry with us, the Oliveira Florencios, because of her own self-interests.

Days later, I called André again. I told him I had received an email that I was sure he and the other brothers and sisters had received as well. Samantha had actually sent it to all the Oliveira Florencios and Santana Florencios. The email said that I, Katia, was preoccupied with the inheritance. I sensed that Samantha was acting unfairly. She had taken documents related to the selling of the lots from David's house without legal consent, and she implied to me on the phone that she would be the one to deal with the lots. Samantha's words on the phone were really clear. That was my understanding.

I really became angry thinking about my conversation with Samantha, as she was trying to buy our brother Eric's trust so she could be in charge of the leftover lots that had to be sold and divided according to the will. She even said in the email that she had an attorney, a friend of hers, who was an ideal person to be in charge of the lots. I thought it was fishy. Actually, the will clearly stated that the Oliveira Florencios, being the children of the married couple of André Florencio and Diana Oliveira Florencio, would receive a higher percentage from the sale of the lots than the Santana Florencios. As I said, this was legally stated. And I believe she knew that.

I came to know that before 1990, before the lots were sold, Samantha had asked David for two lots when she should have had just one, according to the will. She did some business with a construction company, and the owner built her house inside her mother's part of Rancho Aurora. The lots she received from David were located in another area, the first part of my father's ranch.

After André received Samantha's email, he called Ernesto and Eric and told them that he would like to resolve the situation, as Samantha did not have legal consent to deal with our inheritance. André knew that he needed a power of attorney to resolve the situation. Since he lives in Salvador, he was just two hours away from Rancho Aurora in Santana. André contacted our brothers and sisters to get their signatures, giving him authority over the leftover lots to eventually sell them.

André took over resolving issues over the last lots. In the end, the last lots were subdivided accordingly. I guess I should say justice was done and now the angels are at peace with each other. God has a day for everything.

* * *

Time passed by, and one day, the child got a pen and wrote,

So long. See you later, Papa.
—Katia Florencio Parker

www.ingramcontent.com/pod-product-compliance
Lightning Source LLC
LaVergne TN
LVHW041625070526
838199LV00052B/3247